Dinner for One
by Nadine Larsson

*To T.J. and Lisa —
Happy dining together!
Nadine*

Dinner for One

©2012 First Edition
The author reserves all rights.
 No part of this book may be used or reproduced any manner without permission, except in the case of brief quotations embodied in reviews.
ISBN: 978-0-9836310-4-4
If you would like to contact the author, you can write her at
<u>nadine.larsson@gmail.com</u>

Table of Contents

Introduction 1

A Note about Oils 5

A Note about Sea salts 7

Flours to Have on Hand 9

Condiments to Have on Hand 11

Spices to Have on Hand 12

Essential Oils to Have On Hand 13

Biscotti, Dumpling, Fritter and Pancakes 15

    Beet Pancakes with Coconut Sour Cream and Chives 16

    Carrot and Orange Pancakes with Balsamic Reduction Whipped Coconut Cream 18

    Carrot, Pineapple and Toasted Pecan Pancakes with Balsamic Vinegar Reduction 19

    Gluten-Free Dumpling for One 20

    Gluten-Free Pancake Mix 21

    Greens Pancakes 22

    Orange and Cardamom Biscotti 23

    Pepper Biscotti 25

    Raw Beet Pancakes with Oregano and Balsamic Reduction ..26

Zucchini Fritter 27

Salads 29

Apple and Carrot Salad with Toasted Pecans 30

Massaged Kale Salad with Creamy Tahini Miso Dressing 31

Massaged Kale Salad with Tahini and Lemon Dressing 32

Raw Beet and Apple Salad with Pine nuts and Arugula 33

Roasted Beet and Feta Salad 34

Tossed Fall Vegetable Salad 35

Wilted Chard Salad 36

Condiments and Salad Dressings 39

Balsamic Reduction 40

Balsamic Reduction Whipped Coconut Cream 41

Balsamic Vinaigrette 42

Champagne Vinaigrette salad dressing 43

Coconut Sour Cream 44

Cranberry Raisin Chutney 45

Peanut Sauce 46

Sesame Rice Vinaigrette Salad Dressing 47

Beef Entrees 49

Beef Stew for One 50

Cuban Fried Steak (Bistec de Palomilla) 52

Easy Pot Roast for One 54

Orange Beef 55

Skewered Beef..56

Spicy Beef Curry...57

Chicken Entrees..59

Barbecued Chicken Pizza 60

Chicken a l'orange 61

Chicken Cauliflower Curry...62

Chicken Chop Suey 63

Chicken Coconut Curry 64

Chicken Stew with a Dumpling or Two 65

Chinese Style Chicken Chow Mein 67

Chicken Pot Pie...68

Chicken Roll-up with Prosciutto 70

Green Beans with Chicken 71

Is this Beef? Chicken 72

Lemon Chicken 73

Maifun Chicken Salad for One...75

Mediterranean Chicken 76

Murray River Curry 77

Murray River Mediterranean Chicken 79

Quick and Easy Barbecued Chicken 81

Quick and Easy Lemon Baked Chicken 82

Fish, Shellfish, and Mollusk Entrees 85

Baked Salmon with Lemon and Capers 86

Chinese Style Tuna Casserole for One 87

Fried Oysters with Ground Millet Coating 88

Lemony Pancakes with Grilled Shrimp and Lemon Sauce 89

Linguine with Clams 91

Mussels and Chips 92

Poached salmon with Lemon and Capers 93

Steamed Clams with French bread 94

Swordfish with Mango Salsa 95

Tilapia in Panko Crust 96

Pork Entrees 99

Larsson Hash 100

Pork Chop with Cranberry Raisin Chutney 101

Pork Chow Mein 103

Pork Lo Mein 105

- Pork Roast with Mint Rub 106
- Pork Wrap 107
- Simple Pork Ribs 109

Pasta Entrees 111
- Artichoke Hearts, Sun-Dried Tomatoes and Penne 112
- Baked Penne with Kale 113
- Josie Pennello's Unforgettable Spaghetti Sauce 114
- Mac and Cheese for One..116
- Pasta Putanesca..117
- Pasta with Red Pepper and Peas 118
- Pasta with Prosciutto and Peppers....................................119
- Spaghetti Frittata..120

Vegetarian entrees 123
- Beet Green Frittata 124
- Egg Foo Young for One 125
- Gluten-Free Pizza Dough..127
- I Have Too Many Greens This Week Pie 128
- Metropolitan Pizza 130
- Tofu Omelet 131
- Vege Sushi Rolls..132

Vegetable Coconut Curry with Egg 134

Zucchini Parmesan...136

Side dishes 139

Baked Fennel...140

Broccoli Bake 141

Butternut Squash Soufflé for One 142

Cauliflower Steaks 143

Fennel Flavored Risotto for 100 144

Fried Rice...146

Green Beans with Balsamic Finish...147

Greens Sautéed or Steamed with Onion 148

Hasselback Potato 149

Mélange of Root Vegetables with Fennel......................................151

Mélange of Zucchini, Carrot, Beet and Onion.....................153

Oil Me Rosemary Sliced Delicata Squash............................154

Roasted Root Vegetable with Balsamic Reduction 156

Rosemary Potatoes..157

Twice-Baked Potato 158

Zesty Cauliflower 160

Zucchini Chips...161

Soups 163

    Easy Vegetable Soup..164

    Radish Top Soup 165

    Swedish Pasture Soup / Ängemat 166

    White Bean and Kale Soup 167

    White Bean and Pasta Soup 168

101 Dinner Ideas for One 170

Referenced in this Volume..176

Index 177

Introduction

This book is an outgrowth of my book, "Divorce, Empowerment, and Attorneys--What you need to know". I found myself unexpectedly alone after twenty-six years with my handsome and ever-improving, or ever-in-need-of-improvement—your call-- former spouse. I wanted to honor myself, and I wanted to find joy in being alone. Cocooning in my little apartment here in the Stadium District of Tacoma, I've been able to explore myself and my interests, including cooking, in a way I couldn't before. It's been wonderful not having someone judging me, for good or ill—oh, until you. But, I trust you. You'll like some things in this book, and you likely won't like some things in this book—no, that's wrong, YOU are going to LOVE EVERYTHING in this book.

I developed most of these dishes over the past eight years that I've been on my own. Some of them are recipes I adapted from various sources and then combined what I liked into one dish that works for me. Recently, I've had some stomach issues and so I've been exploring gluten-free alternatives. Most of the dishes and meals in this book can be put together in 20-40 minutes. I worked full time with a long daily commute and, although I find cooking to be a good activity for relieving stress, I'd often be too tired to feel like cooking anything at all. So, whatever I was preparing had to be tasty and pretty quick.

Even if I have only a short time in the evening, I want to be swept away with a meal. I want to be my own Scheherazade, transporting myself to a world filled with joy and love. I like candles, and music.

Try putting on some French café music to accompany you while you make Mussels and chips (my version of the French/Belgian Moules Frites), or maybe an Italian Café CD while you make Josie Pennello's Unforgettable Spaghetti Sauce. Sometimes I put those on while I'm cooking to get myself in the mood, and maybe I'll leave them on while I eat and dream of my next attempt at any kind of fiction. Then, sometimes it's just a film. With whom would you like to dine tonight? Clark Gable and Claudette Colbert? Julie Roberts and Hugh Grant? Bring them along, and let's get on with it!

I use mostly chicken because of its low cholesterol. And, because I like simplicity and saving money, I usually buy chicken breasts in those huge packages they sell at Costco and then put them in the freezer where I can take them out one package at a time, and each package has two breasts. The recipes can be adapted for a dinner companion. Some of the recipes, but not all of them, work well when they're doubled. Or, it may be that you're two small eaters. You can add additional sides to make the meal larger, or an appetizer, soup, or desert. And, if you have leftovers, they make a nice lunch the next day.

These meals are intended to be one-offs and not meals that morph into something else, like turkey one evening becomes turkey salad for lunch the next day. I imagine you do that sort of thing without any suggestions from me. No, these are recipes I've adapted from either scratch or from recipes I've found or enjoyed at restaurants. Most of them go from conception to table within thirty minutes--less with a little pre-planning and set up. In the time it takes me to make rice, I've got my main dish ready. I like to assemble all my ingredients at the beginning and I use those little bowls that you see the professional chefs use—I love those little things. I mean, you need to cook anyway; why not have a little fun with it?

Although I think I really have geared this book toward a female audience, it's just as tasty for bachelors as it is for bachelorettes (does anybody still use that term????). Anybody who lives alone and enjoys food, and especially playing with food, will gain something from this book. In fact, there are several recipes that you'll like even if you hate food preparation.

I've incorporated my experiences using Young Living Essential Oils, with gluten-free flours (who knew giving up wheat could be this exciting?), special sea salts (especially sea sea salts), my personal Swedish heritage, and things I've picked up from traveling, into these recipes. Last year found me in Chicago and I was fortunate to be able to dine at a, then, recently opened restaurant called Waffles. I'd never thought of savory waffles before. I don't have the room in my kitchen to house a waffle iron, so I make pancakes instead. And, I do very little dairy so I had to get creative. What you'll find here, then, is something quite unique—a collection of mostly gluten-free, mostly dairy-free, and completely ordinary-free dinners for one.

A Note about Oils

Both olive oil and coconut oil seem to have both their proponents and opponents among health professionals. I use both, but I typically save olive oil to enjoy fresh, uncooked. In my cooking, I use primarily grape seed oil, with some coconut oil and occasional sesame oil thrown in. I use extra virgin olive oil at the end, on fresh or cooked foods, but not in cooking, as a general rule.

When considering using any oil, I want to know:

1. The smoke point. Once any oil begins to smoke, it also begins to lose any healthful properties it may have. In fact, it becomes a poison to your body. I rarely, if ever, use oil containing trans-fats.

2. Whether it is categorized to be "highly beneficial, neutral, or avoid" for my blood type according to the *book Eat Right for Your Blood Type* by Dr. Peter J. D'Adamo with Catherine Whitney. I am type A. Unfortunately, coconut oil is on the "avoid" list for Type A blood, so I try to use it sparingly.

Grape seed oil has a high smoke point (420°). It has been found to raise levels of HDL (good) cholesterol, and to decrease levels of LDL (bad) cholesterol, according to Dr. Ralph Felder, author of "The Bonus Years Diet". It is packed with antioxidants including vitamins C, E and beta-carotene.

Extra virgin coconut oil has a smoke point of 350°. Coconut oil is in the fat category known as MCT or medium chain triglycerides." *MCTs are metabolized differently by your body and provide unique energy-yielding benefits making them a very efficient fuel source. Studies have shown that a diet rich in MCTs can actually support weight loss*" (July 2010 edition of toyourhealth.com).

Sesame oil, unrefined, has a smoke point of 350° and semi-refined has a smoke point of 450°.

Although extra virgin olive oil has a high smoke point of 350° to 400°, with lesser quality olive oils apparently having a lower smoke point, the benefits to the body of both the monounsaturated fats (MUFAs) and the phenols is lost during the cooking process. I've been informed by many nutritionists, and via several articles on the internet (notably, I think one could find support for nearly anything, either side, on the internet), that EVOO is best used without heat. Personally, I enjoy it on salads, and on just about anything in place of butter. Give me a loaf of bread, some balsamic vinegar and olive oil and you won't see me for days. I buy olive oil in the huge cans from my local business Costco. I love the flavor, and it doesn't upset my stomach.

I do occasionally use it in cooking, but very seldom. When I do cook with it, I try to keep the heat to a minimum and add other ingredients to distribute the heat.

A Note about Sea salts

There is a huge difference between refined sea salt and unrefined sea salt. Common table sea salt contains only two elements: sodium and chloride. Natural sea sea salt contains 92 essential minerals. To quote from page 78 of Andreas Moritz in his book, *The Amazing Liver & Gallbladder Flush,*

> *...Refined sea salt...poses a great risk to the body. It prevents this free crossing of liquids and minerals, thereby causing accumulated fluids to stagnate in joints, lymph ducts and lymph nodes and the kidneys. Its dehydrating effect can lead to gallstone formation and numerous other health problems.*
>
> *The body requires sea salt to properly digest carbohydrates. In the presence of natural sea salt, saliva and gastric secretions are readily able to break down the fibrous store of carbohydrates. In its dissolved and ionized form, sea salt facilitates the digestive process and sanitizes the gastro-intestinal tract.*
>
> *In contrast, commercially produced table sea salt has quite the opposite effect. ..After undergoing processing, the sea salt can no longer blend or combine with human body fluids. This invariably undermines the most basic chemical and metabolic processes in the body...*

Andreas Moritz states further on in the same text, "Eating unrefined sea salt fulfills the body's need for sea salt without upsetting the hydro-electrolytic imbalance." He refers to the relatively small amount of sodium in sea sea salt, that this should not be cause for concern when potassium levels in the body are normal. Foods high in potassium include avocados, bananas, beans, potatoes and winter squash. I include some different sea salts in this book and the only source I trust is SaltWorks. For additional information, go to www.SaltWorks.com. I might add, it has been my experience that this company, SaltWorks, has the best customer service department I've ever dealt with—and they are not paying me in any way to do this, it's just the truth, in my experience.

Flours to Have on Hand

For gluten-free cooking and baking, it's handy to have a flour mix and a pancake mix at the ready.

Examples of Whole grain flours:

Amaranth flour
Buckwheat flour (or, buckwheat groats is fine, and then you can just put them in a spice grinder to mill them as needed. They seem to stay fresher that way.)
Millet flour (I buy it whole and mill it at home in a spice grinder)
Quinoa flour
Sorghum flour
Teff flour

Examples of Starches:

Arrowroot flour
Cornstarch
Potato starch flour
Sweet rice flour
Tapioca flour
White rice flour

These flours afford wonderful flexibility and a great change from the one taste of whole wheat. They're a subtle change that can make a big difference in how food tastes.

I learned about flours from Gluten-Free Baking for Dummies®. There's a wealth of information about the subject. I got my basic knowledge there, and now I'm using trial and error for things that work for me and how I bake and cook. I also like the website Gluten-FreeGirlandtheChef.com.

I've made my own mixes for a standard white flour mix to replace the wheat I used to use, and I've made a pancake mix as well. You will find this recipe in the Pancake section of the book. The main thing to keep in mind is: 1) weigh your flours instead of measuring them; and, 2) use a 60/40 ratio, 60% starches to 40% whole grains. Mix whatever flours you want together, just as long as they have that 60% starch and 40% whole grain ratio, and then mix the flours until they're all one color. So, for example, for every 1000 grams, you'll need 600 grams of one or a mixture of flours from the starch group, and 400 grams of one or a mixture of flours from the whole grains group. Mix them together until they're one color and run with it.

You can use regular wheat flour in these recipes, but the instructions for preparation will be different. I've tried to list them in the recipes, but in case they're not there you need to remember that with wheat flour you mix your dry ingredients and wet ingredients separately, and then add your wet to the dry ingredients—and don't over-mix.

Flours can go bad, like any other food. Be sure to keep them from getting moist. I buy small quantities and keep them in the freezer. I keep my everyday flour mix in an airtight container in my pantry, and I store my pre-made pancake mix in the freezer.

Condiments to Have on Hand

Patak's hot curry paste (available online at http://www.ranisworldfoods.com) I have also often found this in local grocery stores, and also available for sale in Indian restaurants

Tamari (wheat free soy sauce, available at all Asian markets, and often available in your local grocery store or in the bulk section of most natural foods stores, or available online at www.**olivenation.com**).

Spices to Have on Hand

Cardamom, ground
Chinese 5-spice powder
Coriander
Cumin
Fresh ginger (You can freeze this and thaw as needed; it re-freezes well, a few times. Keep it in small chunks)
Garam Masala
Mint, dried
Turmeric

Essential Oils to Have On Hand

Fennel
Lemon
Orange
Oregano
Rosemary
Thyme

      The only essential oils I would ever use in cooking, for myself or my family, are those made by Young Living. I've been a distributor for several years now, not because of the business opportunity, but because I enjoy getting my oils at a discount. These are highly concentrated, no nonsense, safe oils that bring a depth of flavor and a convenience to cooking I hadn't enjoyed before finding them. There is a wonderful website, www.youngliving.com, where you can learn more about each of the oils listed above, and more. I don't want to risk any copyright infringement or other error to bring you information about them. You can also order directly from the Young Living site. You're welcome to use my sponsoring distributor number that appears in the back of this book if you wish.

Biscotti, Dumpling, Fritter and Pancakes

Beet Pancakes with Coconut Sour Cream and Chives
Carrot Pancakes with Balsamic Reduction Whipped Coconut Cream
Carrot, Pineapple, and Toasted Pecan Pancakes with Balsamic Vinegar Reduction
Gluten-Free Dumplings
Gluten-Free Pancake Mix
Greens Pancakes
Orange and Cardamom Biscotti
Peppery Biscotti
Raw Beet Pancakes
Zucchini Fritter

Beet Pancakes with Coconut Sour Cream and Chives

Powdered sugar on the top is an excellent choice if you don't have any coconut milk or sour cream handy to go the savory route. A little almond butter on the top and some maple syrup will work too. Serve alongside some bacon or vege bacon strips.

If using wheat flour, mix your dry ingredients and wet ingredients separately, and then add the wet to the dry and stir just until blended. You can let your batter rest, but there is no need to refrigerate it).

1 cup cooked beets
2 eggs
1/2 cup gluten-free pancake mix
1/2 cup mineral water
Sea salt and pepper to taste

1. Put everything into a food processor and process for about 1 minute on low.

2. Put the batter in the refrigerator for about 10-15 minutes while you do something else. I'll often get this ready when I walk in the door and then change to my home clothes while it's in the refrigerator.

3. Pour batter onto a slightly greased cast iron pan preheated to medium or just one step below medium, depending on your pan and stove. Cook for a little less than 2 minutes on each side. You'll know when they're ready to turn or remove from the pan because, as long as you're working with a well- seasoned cast iron pan, the pancakes will not stick and instead easily release. I've found that I can generate the first batch or two on medium heat, and then I need to turn it down to just one notch below medium to keep the pan from smoking.

This recipe makes about 4- 5 4-inch pancakes and I think they're great warmed over too. I just put mine back on the skillet for a few minutes on each side. It may not be "the thing to do", but it works for me.

Serve with Coconut Sour Cream (page 45) and top with chives or thinly sliced scallions.

Of course, you can use regular sour cream—but I prefer this dairy free option.

Carrot and Orange Pancakes with Balsamic Reduction Whipped Coconut Cream

Note: If using a wheat / gluten based pancake mix, mix your dry and your wet ingredients separately and combine by hand just until blended. This recipe was designed to be used with gluten-free pancake mix.

1 carrot, washed and grated (yes, I retain the peels. This should be either 1 large carrot or 2 smaller carrots)
1 egg
1/2 tsp. turbinado sugar
1-2 drops Young Living Essential Oil Orange Oil
1/2 cup mineral water
1/2 cup gluten-free pancake mix
3 Tbs. grape seed oil for frying

1. Put carrot, egg, sugar, essential orange oil, mineral water and pancake mix in a food processor and process for about 1 minute on low.

2. Put the batter in the refrigerator for about 10-15 minutes. This tends to make your gluten-free pancakes a little lighter. Don't bother with this step if you're using wheat; except, when using wheat, your batter will blossom and tend to make fluffier pancakes if you just let it rest on the counter for 10-15 minutes.

3. Heat a cast iron skillet until water sizzles when you put a drop on the skillet. Make sure you give the pancakes room to cook. Brown on both sides, about 2 minutes per side.

4. Top with Balsamic Reduction Whipped Coconut Cream (Page 26).

This recipe makes 3-4 4-inch pancakes and they're great warmed up the next day.

Carrot, Pineapple and Toasted Pecan Pancakes with Balsamic Vinegar Reduction

Note: if for some reason you're using wheat / gluten flour, you will need to mix your wet and your dry ingredients separately and then mix them together but leave some lumps. This recipe was designed to be used with gluten-free pancake mix.

1/2 cup plus 1 Tbs. crushed pineapple with juice
1 large or 2 small carrots, scrubbed but not peeled
1 egg
1/2 tsp. vanilla
1 tsp. sugar
1/2 cup mineral water like Perrier or S. Pellegrino
1/2 cup plus 1 Tbs. gluten-free pancake mix
1/4 cup toasted pecans (to toast, toss over medium heat, stirring constantly, until browned)
3 Tbs. grape seed oil or butter for frying

1. Process the pineapple juice, carrot, egg, vanilla, sugar, mineral water and GF pancake mix in a food processor (isn't that cool??? If you were cooking with wheat flour, you'd have to be careful about the gluten content. With non-wheat-gluten flours, fire away!)

2. Coarsely chop the toasted pecans and add them to your pancake mixture (you can substitute toasted walnut if that's what you have available).

3. Put pancake mixture in the refrigerator for about 10-15 minutes if you have time. You'll find they get fluffier.

4. Heat cast iron skillet over medium heat until a drop of water sizzles when placed on it. Make sure you give the pancakes enough room to branch out and heat through. Brown on both sides and serve. Top with balsamic vinegar reduction or maple syrup, or butter, or powdered sugar and a squeeze of lemon.

Gluten-Free Dumpling for One

You can make this with wheat flour instead of gluten-free flour. In that case, mix your dry ingredients separately from your wet, use milk instead of water, and add the wet ingredients to the dry ingredients. Hand mix, don't put it in a food processor, and let the batter sit on the counter for your 20 minutes. The instructions for this recipe are based on using a gluten-free flour mix. This recipe doubles very well.

This is intended to accompany Chicken Stew with a Dumpling or Two, found on page 65.

1/2 cup gluten free flour mixture
1 Tbs. dried parsley
1/4 tsp. baking powder
1/4 tsp. baking soda
1/4 tsp. sea salt
1 Tbs. extra virgin olive oil
1/3 cup mineral water
1 egg

1. Put all ingredients in a food processor and process on low for about 1 minute or until the dough forms a ball.

2. Put your batter in the refrigerator for about 20 minutes, which is usually enough time to make your chicken stew into which to put your dumplings.

3. When the stew is boiling, add the dumplings and cook, uncovered, for 10 minutes. Then cover and cook for another 10 minutes. Serve.

Gluten-Free Pancake Mix

This is the basic recipe I've been using for pancake mix. I vary it sometimes, depending on what flours I have on hand:

80 grams potato starch (about 1/2 cup)
120 grams cornstarch (about 1 cup)
123 grams quinoa flour (about 1 cup)
250 grams brown rice flour (about 2 cups)
1 Tbs. baking powder
2 tsp. baking soda
1 tsp. sea salt

1. Mix all ingredients together with a wire whisk until the flour is all one color. It's important to mix thoroughly.

2. Store this in an airtight container, or in the freezer. I store mine in plastic freezer bags and reuse the bags. Since you're not actually thawing out the bag itself, there's no change in the composition of the plastic—in case that may be of concern.

Greens Pancakes

Note: if for some reason you're using wheat / gluten flour, you will need to mix your wet and your dry ingredients separately and then mix them together but leave some lumps. Use milk instead of mineral water. This recipe was designed to be used with gluten-free pancake mix.

3 cups greens (beet, chard, kale, or a combination of all three)
1 egg
1/2 cup mineral water
1/2 cup gluten-free pancake mix
1/8 tsp. sea salt

1. Combine all of the ingredients above in a food processor and process until you have a smooth batter, about 1 minute.

2. Put the batter in the refrigerator for about 10-15 minutes.

Heat a cast iron pan over medium heat until a splash of water sizzles on it. Make sure the pancakes have enough room to cook well. Brown them on both sides. Serve.

Try nut butter on these pancakes--peanut butter, almond butter, Tahini/sesame butter--and then drizzle with a little balsamic reduction if you like. Add some caramelized onions maybe, or some chutney, or salsa. Experiment the first time you make this. Explore the taste sensations of what you have on hand.

Orange and Cardamom Biscotti

If using wheat flour, mix your dry ingredients and wet ingredients separately, and then add the wet to the dry and mix well. You can let your dough rest, but there is no need to refrigerate it. This recipe is intended to use with gluten-free flour.

2-1/2 cups gluten-free flour mix
1/2 cup sugar
2 tsp. baking powder
1 tsp. baking soda
1 tsp. sea salt
1/4 cup grape seed or other oil of your choice
3 eggs, separated
1/2 cup mineral water
14 drops Young Living Essential Oils Orange Oil
1-1/2 tsp. cardamom

1. Preheat oven to 350°

2. Put all ingredients except the egg whites together in a food processor (one more time! Can I hear it for gluten free flours???), and then process for about 1 minute or until a dough forms.

3. Beat the egg whites until soft peaks form and fold into the mix.

4. Put the dough in the refrigerator for about 10-15 minutes. Remove to work surface.

5. Divide dough in half and place on a cookie sheet lined with parchment paper, forming two logs about 2-1/2 inches wide and about 1-1/2 inches high. Bake at 350° about 30 minutes. Remove from oven and put the logs on a wire rack to cool.

6. Turn down the oven to 250°.

7. Once the logs are cool, slice them on the diagonal in slices about 1 inch thick. Lay cut side up on a parchment lined cookie sheet and bake at 250° for another 40 minutes. Remove from oven and place on a wire rack to cool (this is very important with gluten free flours).

Pepper Biscotti

If using wheat flour, mix your dry ingredients and wet ingredients separately, and then add the wet to the dry and stir just until blended. You can let your batter rest, but there is no need to refrigerate it.

1 1/2 Tbs. whole black peppercorns
2-1/2 cups gluten free flour
1 tsp. baking powder
1/2 tsp. baking soda
1 tsp. sea salt
1/4 cup grape seed or olive oil
1/2 cup mineral water
3 eggs, separated

1. Preheat oven to 350°.

2. Combine all ingredients except the egg whites in a food processor and process for about 1 minute, or until a dough forms. Beat egg whites to soft peaks, fold in, and put the dough in the refrigerator for about 10-15 minutes.

3. Turn dough out onto work surface and divide down in half.

4. Put on a parchment lined cookie sheet and form the dough into logs about 2-1/2 inches wide and about 1-1/2 inches high.

5. Bake dough in a 350° oven for 40 minutes, or until the logs are golden and firm.

6. Reduce the oven temperature to 250°. Remove logs from oven and place them on a wire rack to cool (this is extremely important when working with gluten-free flours).

7. Once cool, cut logs on the diagonal into slices about 1-1/2 inches thick and back at 250° for another 40 minutes. Place them on a wire rack to cool.

Raw Beet Pancakes with Oregano and Balsamic Reduction

Note: if for some reason you're using wheat / gluten flour, you will need to mix your wet and your dry ingredients separately and then mix them together but leave some lumps. You will also want to use milk instead of mineral water. This recipe was designed to be used with gluten-free pancake mix.

1 cup raw beets, washed and grated (leave the peels on)
1 egg
1/8 tsp. dry oregano or 1 tiny drop of Young Living Essential Oil oregano oil (if insure of intensity, dip a toothpick into the oil, then into the batter)
1/2 cup gluten-free pancake flour
1/2 tsp. turbinado sugar
dash of sea salt
1/2 cup mineral water such as S. Pellegrino or Perrier
2-3 Tbs. grape seed oil or butter for frying

1. Mix all ingredients except the oil or butter for frying in a food processor and process for about 1 minute on low speed.

2. Put the batter in the refrigerator for about 15 minutes to rest. If using wheat flour, let the batter rest on the counter.

3. Drop onto preheated greased cast iron pan and cook for about two minutes on each side. Remove to plate.

Top with Balsamic Reduction if desired. Other topping suggestions are butter and powdered sugar, with or without a squeeze of lemon.

Zucchini Fritter

Note: if for some reason you're using wheat / gluten flour, you will need to mix your wet and your dry ingredients separately and then mix them together but leave some lumps. You will also want to use milk instead of mineral water. This recipe was designed to be used with gluten-free pancake mix.

1 raw zucchini, grated
1 egg
1/2 cup mineral water like S. Pellegrino or Perrier
1/2 cup gluten-free pancake mix
1/8 tsp. sea salt
Grape seed oil or butter for frying

1. Combine all of the ingredients above, except for the grape seed oil or butter to be used for frying. Let the mixture sit for 10-20 minutes in the refrigerator to develop.

2. Heat a cast iron pan over medium heat until you can sprinkle water on it and the water instantly bubbles. Add the batter, one pancake at a time, and spread it out a little so it cooks evenly. Cook about 2 minutes on each side. Remove to serving plate.

I like mine plain, maybe with some sea salt and pepper. You can also top it with some salsa, or some spaghetti sauce, or just some extra virgin olive oil, or butter. Or, with Coconut Sour Cream whose recipe can be found on page 44 of this cookbook.

Salads

Apple and Carrot Salad with Toasted Pecans
Massaged Kale Salad with Creamy Tahini Miso Dressing
Massaged Kale Salad with Tahini and Lemon Dressing
Raw Beet and Apple Salad with Pine Nuts and Arugula
Roasted Beet and Feta Salad
Tossed Fall Vegetable Salad
Wilted Chard Salad

Apple and Carrot Salad with Toasted Pecans

This is nice to go along with a simple chicken breast that you've put into the oven for exactly 20 minutes at 350°. Or, with a pork chop you've browned on both sides and then heated, covered, for 4 minutes on each side.

1 apple, peeled and chopped or grated
1 carrot, washed/scraped and finely diced or grated
1/4 cup chopped dry roasted pecans (more like 1/3 cup dry, before roasting or chopping)
Dusting of sea sea salt on the pecans
2 Tbs. champagne vinegar
1 Tbs. extra virgin olive oil
Sea salt and pepper, if desired

1. Roast the pecans over medium high heat in a dry skillet, shaking the pan constantly.

2. Mix all of the ingredients together in a bowl and adjust seasonings if using. Let this sit for a few minutes for the flavors to meld if you can.

Massaged Kale Salad with Creamy Tahini Miso Dressing

This recipe is adapted from a recipe I found at cookieandkate.com.

This is also tasty with toasted pine nuts, tamari roasted pumpkin seeds, or toasted slivered almonds.

1 bunch raw kale, cleaned and drained
1/4 cup Tahini
1 Tbs. miso
1-1/2 Tbs. rice vinegar
1/2 tsp. toasted sesame oil
Pinch red pepper flakes
1/3 cup water
1 tsp. tamari

1. Cut the ribs from the kale. I usually use a pair of scissors for this, or pull it away by hand. Discard the stems, or use them in a broth you make once a week from cleaned and leftover vegetable peelings. Slice in ribbons and set aside.

2. Put all the other ingredients into a food processor and process until smooth. Taste.

3. Adjust seasonings as required (I don't usually have to do anything with this one) to suit your personal taste.

4. Pour the dressing over the kale and literally massage it into the greens, breaking down the kale.

Massaged Kale Salad with Tahini and Lemon Dressing

Here's one more version of a massaged kale salad that I found at Federated Media Publishing Food. The name of the recipe I adapted is Kale Salad with a Tahini-Lemon Dressing, posted by Lauren Ziewtsman on June 22, 2012.

Kale is so good for you, and it's so easy to work with. I vary it between this recipe below and the one on the previous page. I really like the lemony part, and this one goes really well with the tilapia recipe on page 96.

1 bunch kale, cleaned and drained
1/4 cup Tahini
1/2 cup lemon juice
1 Tbs. lemon zest
1 tsp. sea salt
2 Tbs. water

1. Put all the ingredients except the kale into a food processor and process until creamy. Thin with additional water as necessary.

2. Remove the kale stems and toss or use in your weekly vegetable broth and chop the kale leaves.

3. Massage the dressing into the kale and serve immediately or let it sit.

I've let this sit in the refrigerator for up to a week and it's still been wonderful.

Raw Beet and Apple Salad with Pine nuts and Arugula

I toast my pine nuts in a skillet over medium heat, twirling, shaking or stirring until they're just the right hint of toasty brown.

1 fresh beet, peeled and chopped
1 apple, cored, peeled, and chopped
2 Tbs. pine nuts, toasted
Small handful of arugula, if available
Reduced balsamic vinegar

1. Mix beet, apple, pine nuts and arugula in a bowl.

2. Drizzle the reduced balsamic over them. Serve.

Roasted Beet and Feta Salad

Beets, oven roasted, cooled and peeled—or, boiled and peeled works too
Red onion
Feta cheese crumbles
Champagne vinaigrette
Sea salt and pepper to taste

1. Please don't use canned beets. It's simple to roast beets at 400° for 45-60 minutes, depending on size, let them cool. Remove the skins. The skins come off pretty easily, and if any remains, it's tasty too. If you have beets left over that you're not using in salad, you can put them in a 30/70 mixture of vinegar and water, with a little sugar and you'll have some delightful pickled beets to enjoy with other meals.

2. Slice as much red onion as you feel like (date night--blind or planned?) in paper thin slices, arrange them on top of the beets, and then add the feta cheese crumbles.

3. Add some champagne vinaigrette salad dressing (recipe on page 43) a light touch of a nice little sea salt and some freshly ground black pepper. Serve.

Tossed Fall Vegetable Salad

This salad is great for lunches because it needs no refrigeration. It goes great with everything. You can serve it with fish and toss on a little lemon juice. You can serve it with pork chops and toss a touch of tamari over it. You can serve it warm and add a drizzle of extra virgin olive oil. You can add some fresh red or white onion.

1 cup cauliflower, chopped
1 cup broccoli, chopped
1 carrot, scrubbed/scraped and chopped
2 Tbs. extra virgin olive oil
1/2 tsp. or to taste of Fleur de Sel Artisan Sea salts from SaltWorks
Pepper to taste

1. Heat water in a 3-1/2 quart saucepan to boiling. Blanch the vegetables for 3 minutes and drain. You can retain the liquid for your weekly vegetable broth if you like.

2. Toss with the olive oil and the sea salt. Serve immediately or let it sit at room temperature for as much as a couple of hours, or in the refrigerator overnight.

Wilted Chard Salad

1 slice prosciutto, cut into 1/8 inch strips
1/4 medium onion
2 Tbs. water
3 cups Swiss chard, cleaned, drained and cut into ribbons (you can also use kale)
1 Tbs. Apple cider vinegar
1 Tbs. extra virgin olive oil
Sea salt and pepper

1. In a large skillet, heat the prosciutto, dry, over medium heat.
2. Add the onion. Be brave. You haven't added any oil, but that's going to be okay.
3. Now that the onions are starting to get a little brown, add the water and the vinegar and immediately add the Swiss chard. Cover skillet with a tight fitting lid.
4. Cook just until the chard is wilted. Remove from heat.
5. Add the olive oil. Toss. Add a finishing touch of freshly ground black pepper and Murray River flake sea salt.

Condiments and Salad Dressings

Balsamic Reduction Whipped Coconut Cream
Balsamic Vinaigrette
Balsamic Vinegar Reduction
Champagne Vinaigrette
Coconut Sour Cream
Cranberry Raisin Chutney
Peanut Sauce
Sesame Rice Vinaigrette

Balsamic Reduction

To make reduced balsamic vinegar, boil about two cups of balsamic vinegar until it reduces to about a half cup. You can add fruit juice to it if you want some kind of flavoring, like apple or pear juice.

I remember going to dinner with my colleagues at the last company for which I worked when the owner and his wife came to visit. It was at a lovely restaurant in Seattle's Magnolia neighborhood. They served a Caprese Salad with passion fruit infused balsamic reduction and coarse sea sea salt. I thought about how they probably made the balsamic reduction and then I tried out my idea. It tasted great and I've used it from time to time ever since. I really enjoy the distinctive taste of just the plain reduced balsamic, without any added juices. It adds a nice little hint of sweet that plays off the sea salt. It's music to your mouth.

Balsamic Reduction Whipped Coconut Cream

There are two schools of thought here. *You can either go sweet or savory. For sweet, mix in 1 tsp. vanilla extract in place of the balsamic reduction called for in this recipe. For savory, follow the instructions as is.

1 can coconut milk, full fat, chilled overnight
2 Tbs. powdered sugar
2 tsp. balsamic reduction, or 1 tsp. vanilla extract*

1. Carefully spoon out the top layer of opaque white stuff that has gathered at the top of the can of coconut milk into a mixing bowl. (With the *Extra Rich and Creamy* variety from Trader Joe's, it's actually easier to turn the can upside down and take out the liquid first, then open the other side and shove the cream out the other end.)

2. Add 2 Tbsp. of powdered confectioner's sugar to the white stuff.

3. Whip the coconut milk until creamy. You seem to get the best blending by using the lowest speed on your mixer. Just let it go on its own for about 5 minutes. If you can, move the beater in an up and down motion to infuse the mixture with as much air as possible.

4. Beat in your flavor of choice and serve. You could also add a different extract or essential oil. You could add some lemon, or orange, oil, just a drop, instead of, or in addition to, the vanilla.

Balsamic Vinaigrette

1/4 cup balsamic vinegar
1/4 cup cold pressed extra virgin olive oil
Pinch of sea salt
2 tsp. raw or turbinado sugar

Shake until mixture is combined. If you like garlic, mince a clove and add that if you like.

Champagne Vinaigrette Salad Dressing

1/4 cup champagne vinegar
2 tsp. raw or turbinado sugar
1/4 cup cold pressed extra virgin olive oil
Pinch of sea salt

Assemble ingredients in a small bowl, jar or bottle, and stir or shake vigorously. That's it! You're done. Pour it on something and enjoy.

Coconut Sour Cream

Now that I've found this delicious addition, I keep a can of full fat coconut in my refrigerator all the time so I'm always prepared when I'm in the mood for either the coconut sour cream or the whipped cream. I've found the Thai Kitchen unsweetened first pressing coconut milk to have a creamy consistency and be excellent for this application.

1 can Thai Kitchen unsweetened first pressing coconut milk, chilled (Trader Joe's Extra Thick and Rich Coconut Cream is also good)
3 tsp. white vinegar

1. Chill coconut cream overnight.

2. Open the can and remove the gelled "cream" at the top of the can (with the Trader Joe's variety, it's easier to turn the can upside down, pour off the liquid, and then remove the other end and push the "cream" out). Mix the two together with a hand mixer, moving the hand mixer up and down to add as much air as possible. You can serve immediately, but it's better after it sits for an hour or so, or overnight in the refrigerator. I've done it both ways. The taste morphs and mellows just a little—I like it both ways.

Cranberry Raisin Chutney

You can also make this little chutney ahead of time in larger batches and keep it in the refrigerator. It should keep in the refrigerator for two to three weeks.

1 Tbs. balsamic vinegar
1 small pinch red pepper flakes or to suit your taste
1/4 tsp. cumin
3 tsp. turbinado sugar
3 Tbs. water
3 Tbs. dried cranberries
3 Tbs. raisins
3 Tbs. finely diced red onion

1. Heat small saucepan over medium heat.

2. Add the balsamic vinegar.

3. Add the red pepper flakes and cumin and let the spices develop for maybe 30 seconds.

4. Add the sugar, stirring constantly. Add the water, cranberries, raisins and red onion. Let these cook a little over medium heat. Serve.

Peanut Sauce

1/4 cup peanut butter, creamy or crunchy—your call
1/4 cup water
1 Tbs. lime juice
1/4 tsp. ground cumin
1/4 tsp. ground coriander
Dash sea salt
Small pinch red pepper flakes, if desired
1 clove garlic, minced, if desired

Warm all ingredients together over medium heat, stirring constantly to mix ingredients, until mixture is warm and smooth. Use this to dip your wraps (page 107) in. If you have any leftovers (unlike me) they'll keep in the refrigerator for a few days, or you can put them in the freezer for a month or so.

If you have some extra peanuts lying about, especially those wonderful old fashioned blister peanuts from Trader Joe's, you can coarsely grind up a few of those in your spice grinder to drizzle over the top of your wraps.

Sesame Rice Vinaigrette Salad Dressing

1/4 cup rice vinegar
1 tsp. raw or turbinado sugar
2 Tbs. sesame oil
Pinch of sea salt

Shake until mixture is combined.

Beef Entrees

Beef Stew for One
Cuban Fried Steak
Easy Pot Roast
Orange Beef
Skewered Beef
Spicy Beef Curry

Beef Stew for One

4-6 ounce chuck steak, cut into bite sized pieces
1/4 cup buckwheat flour to dust the beef
2 Tbs. grape seed oil for frying the beef
Vegetables*
1/4 cup dry red wine, sweet vermouth or beef stock
2-1/2 cups Beef or vegetable stock (I usually use Better than Bullion combined with water)|
1 tsp. cornstarch dissolved in 3 Tbs. water

1. Marinade the beef in:

1/4 cup olive oil
Juice of one lemon
1 or 2 cloves garlic if desired
Sea salt and pepper

You can put beef in a dish or in a plastic freezer bag to marinate. Marinate the beef anywhere from 30 minutes to 24 hours. Remove and cut into bite size chunks.

2. Dust beef with flour, sauté in fresh oil. I usually toss out the marinade, but you can add it to your stew if you like since you're going to boil it to remove any bacteria.

3. Deglaze with a little red wine, sweet vermouth or beef stock.

4. Add your vegetables.*This depends on what vegetables you have on hand, and on how hungry you are. Suggestions are:
1 carrot, cut into bite sized chunks
1 stalk celery, cut into bite sized chunks
1 small potato, peeled or not, whichever your preference is, and cut into bite sized chunks|
1 turnip, cut into bite sized chunks
A handful of kale
1/2 onion, or one whole onion, depending on your preference, cut into bite sized chunks

Let the vegetables cook until they've been allowed to sweat a little and become tender.

5. Add remaining beef or vege stock, bring to a boil. Boil 10-15 minutes and then add your cornstarch mixture. Stir and allow your stew to thicken, and serve.

Cuban Fried Steak (Bistec de Palomilla)

Adapted from Memories From a Cuban Kitchen *by Mary Urrutia Randelman and Joan Schwartz*

4-6 ounce top round steak, pounded to about 1/4 inch thick
1 clove garlic, chopped (optional)
Juice of 1 lime
2 Tbs. olive oil
Sea salt and freshly ground pepper to taste
2 Tbs. grape seed oil for frying
1/2 medium sized onion, finely chopped
1/2 cup fresh parsley, cleaned, dried (it is a must that this parsley be totally free of moisture—that is the secret to this dish) and finely chopped

1. Pound the steak. Season with the garlic, the lime juice and the sea salt and pepper and allow it to marinate for at least an hour in the refrigerator. I've put this together in a morning or on the night before and then prepared it after work.

2. Remove the steak from the marinade and shake off excess marinade. In a cast iron frying pan, heat the oil over medium high heat until quite hot and brown the steak for about 2 – 3 minutes on each side.

3. Transfer the steak to your dinner plate and keep warm.

4. Cook the onion just until browned and top the steak.

5. Cook the parsley over medium high heat. It will turn crispy. Stay with it, don't leave it, and when it's just browned and crispy, add it to your steak topping.

6. Now, add the marinade to your pan and using a metal spatula get as much of whatever is left over in the pan by way of sediment as you can. Pour this over your steak.

Now, what I really like to serve with this is: white rice (okay, shoot me—yes, I adore white rice, in moderation) and warmed up black beans (I use the ones in the can, drain them and rinse them). And, last, but not least, I adore this dish with a plantain—a ripe plantain, sliced and fried. I swear to you: this is better than sex. Feel free to write me about your experience.

If you really want to have a cool Cuban experience, enjoy this with a daiquiri: 2 ounce Bacardi light rum, 1 ounce fresh lime juice, 3 tsp. sugar, 1/2 cup crushed ice. Toss that in your blender or food processor, pour into a chilled glass and garnish with a lime slice.

Easy Pot Roast for One

You can put this in your slow cooker, or in the oven, or in a pressure cooker. I usually get stuck with the oven just because I don't have room for a slow cooker anymore.

4-6 ounce chuck steak
1/2 orange, zest and juice, or 8-10 drops Young Living Essential Orange Oil
1/2 onion, thickly sliced
2 Tbs. grape seed oil or butter
1 or 2 whole carrots, depending on how you feel
1 small or medium potato, cut in half
1/4 cup dry red wine

1. You can add one of whatever other vegetable you like, like a little turnip, or rutabaga, for example.

2. Heat a cast iron skillet over medium high heat. Add the oil and sear the steak on each side.

3. Add all the other ingredients and bake at 350° for 45 minutes while you stretch, do some yoga or maybe take an Epsom sea salt bath.

Orange Beef

4-6 ounce 1 round steak, or chuck steak, whichever you prefer, thinly sliced

For the marinade:
8 – 10 drops Young Living Essential Orange Oil
1 Tbs. rice wine vinegar
1 Tsp. tamari
1 Tbs. Mirin or sake
3 Tbs. water or orange juice
1 Tbs. turbinado sugar
1 Tbs. fresh ginger, minced
1 tsp. Chinese five spice powder

Other ingredients:
1/4 cup sweet brown rice flour to lightly dust beef
1 Tbs. grape seed oil
1 Tbs. sesame oil
1 small zucchini, diced
1/2 red or yellow pepper, diced
1/2 small onion or 1/4 large onion, diced

1. Mix marinade ingredients together and marinate beef overnight.

2. Remove beef from marinade and shake off excess. Lightly dust in the flour.

3. Heat frying pan over medium high heat, add grape seed and sesame oil and brown beef on both sides.

4. Add zucchini, pepper and onion. Cook through.

5. Add remaining marinade to the vegetables and beef and cook just until the liquid has reduced.

I like this with brown jasmine rice, or sometimes I'll just have a serving of greens with it.

Skewered Beef

4 ounce top round or sirloin steak, cut into bite size pieces
1 Tbs. melted butter or grape seed oil
6 whole cherry tomatoes
1 zucchini, sliced about 1" thick
4 whole mushrooms or mushroom caps
1/2 or whole onion, depending on size of onion and your personal taste preference, cut into big chunks
1 Tbs. Reduced balsamic vinegar for glazing afterward
2 long metal skewers

1. Thread ingredients onto metal skewers, alternating. If you like your beef very well done, you may want to have the meat on a separate skewer from veges.

2. Preheat broiler.

3. Brush filled skewers with melted butter or grape seed oil and broil until the beef is done and the vegetables are browned. Remove from the broiler and brush immediately with the balsamic glaze.

You can also add a skewer of boiled potato, cut into chunks, if you want a starch. Or, serve this with a side of greens, or rice, or both.

Spicy Beef Curry

You can turn this into a one dish meal by adding a cold potato, diced, and a sliced carrot and/or a sliced zucchini.

Patak's hot beef curry paste – about 1 tsp. or to taste
2 Tbs. grape seed oil
1/4 cup quinoa flour to dust beef and retain the moisture
4 ounces top round or sirloin steak, cut into bite sized pieces
1/2 onion, sliced
1 cup water or stock
Sea salt and pepper to taste

1. Dust beef with flour—put it on a paper towel and then toss the excess easily.

2. Heat cast iron skillet over medium high heat, add grape seed oil, then beef. Brown beef on both sides, add the onion and cook onion until just browned. Reduce heat to medium.

3. Add the curry paste, cook about 30 seconds to allow the paste to warm. Add the water or stock and cook, uncovered, until water has reduced by at least half. Serve.

Serve this with Major Grey's Chutney (or the Cranberry Raisin Chutney from page 45) and white or brown basmati rice.

This is also great when you replace the grape seed oil with coconut oil and add a side of sliced banana.

Chicken Entrees

Barbecued Chicken Pizza
Chicken a l'orange
Chicken Cauliflower Curry
Chicken Chop Suey
Chicken Coconut Curry
Chicken Pot Pie
Chicken Roll Up with Prosciutto
Chicken Stew with a Dumpling or Two
Chinese Style Chicken Chow Mein
Green Beans with Chicken
Is This Beef? Chicken
Lemon Chicken
Maifun Chicken Salad for One
Mediterranean Chicken
Murray River Curry
Murray River Mediterranean Chicken
Quick and Easy Barbecued Chicken
Quick and Easy Lemon Baked Chicken

Barbecued Chicken Pizza

I'm not eating much cheese lately, or any kind of dairy, so I didn't put any cheese on this pizza. It is, however, a pizza—put on it what you like. This may just be a jumping off point for you.

1 skinless chicken breast, chopped into small, bite-sized pieces
1/4 cup quinoa flour
1 pizza crust (see page 127)
2 Tbs. grape seed oil
2 Tbs. catsup
1/2 tsp. Worcestershire sauce or 1 tsp. Bragg's Liquid Aminos
Dash sea salt
1/2 tsp. turbinado sugar
1/4 cup red onion, thinly sliced
5 kalamata olives, sliced
1 small zucchini, thinly sliced

1. Preheat oven to 350°.

2. Mix the catsup, Worcestershire sauce, sugar and sea salt. Let it sit while you cook the chicken so the flavors can meld.

3. Heat a skillet on medium high heat. Add the grape seed oil.

4. Dredge the chicken pieces in the quinoa flour by putting the flour onto a paper towel. Brown the chicken pieces on each side and then add the catsup mixture. Turn heat to low and allow the chicken to sit in the sauce while you prepare your crust.

5. Roll out the pizza dough. Add the chicken and catsup mixture and distribute the catsup mixture across the pizza.

6. Add the red onion, olives and zucchini.

7. Bake at 350° for 12 minutes and serve.

Chicken a L'Orange

This is wonderful with a wild rice accompaniment. You can get really fancy and add 1/4 cup of an orange liqueur and set the dish aflame, then serve. Usually, though, I'm so tired I just want to see and smell something wonderful on the table in front of me without a whole lot of fuss and bother. But, sometimes, like on a lonely weekend, I really do enjoy sitting with an old movie and maybe having one dry martini before, then this great dish with the wild rice on the side, and then I'll do a little flambé. It's fun, and it reminds me I can still handle even the wildest gourmet, should he show up on my doorstep.

1 chicken breast, skinless and boneless, chopped into large bite-sized pieces
1/4 cup potato flour
2 Tbs. tapioca flour
15 drops Orange oil by Young Living Essential Oils
1/4 cup red onion, thinly sliced
2 Tbs. grape seed oil
Pinch red pepper flakes

1. Heat pan over medium high heat.

2. Combine potato and tapioca flour on a paper towel and dredge the chicken to coat on all sides.

3. Add the grape seed oil to the pan, then the red pepper flakes, and then add the chicken. Brown the chicken on both sides and then add the red onion. Cover and cook ten minutes or until chicken is done. Serve.

Chicken Cauliflower Curry

If you enjoy things that are a little spicy, you can add some red pepper flakes. You can also replace the chicken stock with a cup of coconut milk, add a hardboiled egg, and make it a little spicier with a fresh chili pepper. Play with this. Get creative. It's about you and bringing your taste buds to life again!

1 chicken breast, cut into bite sized pieces and dredged lightly in flour
1/2 onion
1 cup chicken stock
2 tsp. garam masala
1 tsp. turmeric
1 tsp. fresh ginger, chopped
1 cup (or more, if you like) cauliflower
2 Tbs. grape seed or coconut oil

1. Heat skillet to where it's too hot to put your finger in it, and then add the oil.

2. Add the garam masala, ginger, and the turmeric and let them kind of heat up a bit, for about thirty seconds, then add your onion. Cook for 1-2 minutes, just to give the onions a head start.

3. Lastly, add the chicken breast. Brown on two sides, then add the chicken stock and cauliflower and cook on medium heat for about another 7-10 minutes.

If you like, maybe add a small side salad to this, with just a little fresh lettuce or whatever you have on hand, and dress it with a little champagne or sesame vinaigrette.

Chicken Chop Suey

I serve rice with this, and that's it. If I have someone to dinner, I'll add a tossed salad of some kind, especially with a little arugula added, and toss it with sesame rice vinaigrette dressing (page 47).

1 chicken breast, cut into large bite sized pieces
Flour to dust chicken with, about ½ cup – amaranth is great
1/2 cup onion, sliced lengthwise
1/2 red bell pepper
1 or more stock broccoli, sliced diagonally
1/4 tsp. Chinese five spice powder
1 Tbs. sesame oil
1 small summer squash or zucchini, about ½ - 1 cup
1/4 cup tamari

1. Slice up your chicken and dust it with flour.

2. Slice up your vegetables, either the ones mentioned in this recipe or you can substitute these with whatever you have in your refrigerator. You'll want about three cups of veges.

3. Heat a wok or skillet on medium high heat, add sesame oil, and then add your chicken. Brown the chicken on one side and turn over. Brown the other side of the chicken for about thirty seconds, and then add your vegetables.

4. Just toss the veges over the top of the chicken along with the five spice powder and let the tastes mingle a little while the chicken finishes cooking, about another five minutes.

5. Add the tamari. Give this a stir and cook just until the vegetables are crisp/tender, about another minute. Remove from heat, dust with roasted sesame seeds and serve.

Chicken Coconut Curry

I like to have this with the Apple Raisin Chutney in this cookbook, or with Major Grey's Chutney. I often cook rice to serve alongside, and it's also tasty with some sliced potato that you par-boil with the carrots.

1 chicken breast, cut into bite sized pieces
Quinoa flour
1/2 - 1 Tbs. Patak's hot curry paste, depending on your personal taste
1 cup coconut milk (you can add more depending on your tastes and what you have on hand)
3 small carrots, coarsely chopped and par-boiled
1/4 medium onion, coarsely chopped
1 Tbs. grape seed oil

1. Put the chopped carrots in a large skillet along with just enough water to cover. Boil just until the carrots are crisp tender. Drain.

2. Bring skillet up to temp again over medium / medium high heat. Add the grape seed oil.

3. Dredge chicken pieces in flour and brown on one side, and then turn pieces over and add the chopped onion. Cook until the onion is tender and the chicken has browned on the second side.

4. Add the curry paste and let it warm a little. Add the carrots. Add the coconut milk. Let this simmer for about 10 minutes and serve.

Chicken Stew with a Dumpling or Two

Who doesn't love a warm stew on a cold night? The gluten free dumplings on page 20 go together super quickly and, topping this dish, make you feel like the great earth mother is giving you a big warm hug. Snuggle up.

1 chicken breast, cut into bite size pieces
1/4 cup millet flour to dust chicken to retain moisture
2 Tbs. grape seed oil
Small pinch of red pepper, if desired
1 clove minced garlic, if desired
2 Tbs. fresh parsley, if available, or 1 Tbs. dried parsley
2 stalks celery, sliced
1/2 medium onion, finely chopped
1 carrot, sliced thinly
1/4 tsp. dried thyme, 1 sprig of fresh thyme or 1 drop Young Living Essential Thyme Oil
1/4 tsp. dried rosemary, 1 small sprig of fresh rosemary, or 1 drop Young Living Essential Rosemary Oil
3 cups Chicken stock
Fleur de Sel sea salt by Artisan Sea salt Company available from SaltWorks
Ground pepper to taste

You'll need about a 3 or 3-1/2 quart covered saucepan for this. You need some room for the dumpling to rise.

1. Prepare your dumplings (page 20) and let them sit while you prepare your stew.

2. Dust the chicken with the flour and set aside. Prepare your vegetables and have them standing by.

2. Heat your saucepan over medium/medium high heat, add the grape seed oil, then the red pepper and the garlic if using.

3. Add the chicken to the grape seed oil and brown on both sides.

4. Once browned, add the parsley, celery, onion and carrot, and the thyme UNLESS you are using Thyme essential oil. Cook over medium heat until the vegetables are just cooked through.

5. Add the chicken broth. Add the sea salt and pepper. NOW you can add the thyme and rosemary essential oils. Cover and cook stew for 5-10 minutes before adding dumplings.

6. Bring to a boil and add the dumplings. Cook uncovered for 10 minutes. Cover and cook another 10 minutes. Serve.

Chinese Style Chicken Chow Mein

I like to have this with either brown or purple rice. It's a one dish meal, so what's not to like? Maybe create your space by putting on an old movie like Soldier of Fortune with Susan Hayward and Clark Gable, or the original version of Shall We Dance—or the CD of the Silk Road Project.

1 chicken breast, cut into bite sized pieces
1/2 cup crispy noodles
1/2 onion, sliced
2 Tbs. Tamari
1 Tbs. oyster sauce
2 Tbs. mirin (sweet rice wine)
 Vegetables of your choosing. I usually add a cup or more, depending on how hungry I am, of whatever's in season. In the summer and fall, it's sliced summer squash, and in the winter it's maybe broccoli, or cauliflower, daikon or frozen peas. Sometimes I'll add bamboo shoots or water chestnuts, but I really only like a little of those and I don't like to waste. It just depends on how I feel and what I already have on hand.
1 stalk celery, sliced
2 Tbs. grape seed oil
1/4 cup flour for lightly dusting the chicken

1. Whisk together the tamari, oyster sauce and mirin set aside.

2. Lightly dust the chicken with flour. Heat your skillet, or wok, on as high a heat as the pan can handle. Add the grape seed oil, then the chicken.

3. Brown the chicken briefly and add the onion. Brown and toss for about one minute, then add vegetables. Cook another minute.

4. Add the crispy noodles. Serve.

Chicken Pot Pie

This is either a weekend meal, or one that you might want to prepare the night before you're going to want it and then either cook it and warm it up the next day, or get it ready to bake and bake it the evening you're going to eat it, especially if you're making the pie crust from scratch—and I hope you do.

Pie sauce:

1 chicken breast, cut into small bite sized chunks
Millet flour (I buy millet at Marlene's and grind it in a spice grinder)
2 Tbs. grape seed oil
Tiny pinch red pepper flakes
1/2 tsp. dried thyme, or 1 tsp. fresh thyme, or 10 drops Young Living Essential thyme oil
1/2 – 1 small potato, cooked (I use leftover potato when I have it), diced
1 carrot, brushed and diced
1 stalk celery, cleaned and diced
1/4 onion, diced
Small handful frozen peas
2 Tbs cornstarch dissolved in 1/4 cup cold water
1/2 cup chicken stock (I usually use Better than Bullion from Costco)
Parsley, either 1 Tbs. dry parsley, or 2 Tbs. fresh
Deglaze with 2 Tbs. dry vermouth if you feel like it before adding the chicken stock

1. Heat oven to 350°

2. Dust the chicken breast with the milled millet flour.

3. Heat skillet over medium/medium high heat, add oil, then the cayenne, then the chicken. Brown on both sides. Turn heat to medium.

4. Add the vegetables – except the frozen peas -- and the spices. Cook until the vegetables have sweated/just cooked through.

5. Add the chicken broth and corn starch mixture, and cook just until reduced. You should have a nice little thick sauce, not too runny, and not like glue either, just nice, and flavorful.

6. Add the chicken and sauce to the pie crust and bake at 350° for 20 minutes (depending on your oven).

Pie crust:

You can use a prepared crust, or the following recipe:

1 cup flour (either unbleached white flour, whole wheat flour, or the white flour mixture that's gluten-free from this book or some other book)
1/2 cup shortening, olive oil, or butter
1/4 cup mineral water

If using wheat flour, cut the shortening into the flour until the mixture looks like fine crumbs. If using gluten-free flour you can just toss all of this into a food processer because – that's right – there is no gluten to worry about disturbing. If using wheat flour, add the mineral water at the end. Actually, if using wheat flour, you can use regular water just fine. The mineral water is a plus for the gluten-free flour.

Chicken Roll-up with Prosciutto

I like to enjoy this with a nice crisp salad, or some cooked greens. A little cooked pasta is nummy with this too. It sort of depends on what kind of mood I'm in. Do I want to eat skinny and healthy? Or, do I want to indulge a little? If I want to indulge, then it's the penne or spaghetti on the side topped with a touch of olive oil and a little sea salt (I like Fusion Black Truffle Sea Sea salt from Artisan Sea salts, available from Sea salt Works) and pepper. Mostly, I remember myself on the dance floor and think how much easier it is for me to do spins and turns when I've enjoyed a nice crisp salad. Sometimes the dancer wins, sometimes not.

1 chicken breast, pounded to 1/4" thickness
1 slice Prosciutto
 tsp. dried parsley or 2 tsp. fresh parsley
Quinoa flour for dusting to retain moisture
2 Tbs. grape seed oil

1. Pound the chicken breast, lay it flat and put the slice of Prosciutto on the top. Roll it up keep it closed with a couple of toothpicks or metal skewers. Roll it in flour to hold in the moisture.

2. Heat the oil in a skillet. Brown the chicken on both sides and cover. Let cook about 5 – 7 minutes and you're done.

A baked potato is great with this too, especially organic red potatoes. Put a little grape seed oil in an oven safe dish, place the potato cut side down and bake it in a 350-400° oven for about 20 minutes.

Green Beans with Chicken

1/4 cup Quinoa flour, less 2 Tbs.
2 Tbs. Potato flour
1 Chicken breast, boned and cut into chunks
1/4 Onion, thinly sliced
2 Tbs. Rice wine vinegar
1 Tsp. Sesame oil plus 1 Tbs. grape seed oil, for frying
1 cup Green beans, fresh

1. Mix the potato flour and the quinoa flour together in a small bowl, or use a paper towel you can toss afterwards. Coat your chicken and have it ready.

2. Heat pan over medium high heat, add sesame oil and grape seed oil, then the chicken. Brown chicken on both sides, then add the onion and the green beans, and cover.

3. Cook for another five to seven minutes, remove cover and deglaze pan with the rice wine vinegar. Serve.

Is this Beef? Chicken

The name comes from the way the buckwheat flour looks after it's cooked.

2 Tbs. grape seed oil
1 chicken breast, cut into chunks
Buckwheat flour
Cauliflower, about a cup
1/2 red bell pepper
1 green onion
1/4 cup white wine

1. Coat the chicken with the buckwheat flour.

2. Heat skillet over medium high heat and add the oil. Add the chicken and brown on both sides.

3. Add the onion and the cauliflower. Cover. Cook five minutes.

4. Add the bell pepper. Cook, uncovered, another two minutes.

5. Deglaze by pouring the white wine in the pan and getting all the nummy bits from the bottom. Serve.

Lemon Chicken

This dish was inspired by my friend Denise Belanger and by one of our favorite restaurants, Marzano's, in Tacoma.

I find that a brief dusting of flour tends to keep the chicken more moist. It's really handy to use a paper towel to put the flour on so you can just throw the mess away and not have an extra dish to clean up. I also find it helpful, and fun, to gather and measure out my ingredients ahead of time. It feels like it keeps my mind more orderly somehow. As for chicken broth, I've been buying the Better Than Bouillon from Costco. It's a paste that comes in a jar you keep in the refrigerator and use as needed. For this recipe, I use one teaspoon paste in a cup of boiling water. I use white pepper for this recipe, and Snowflake® Pacific Northwest Sea Sea salt by Artisan Sea salts available from Sea salt Works.

1 chicken breast, sliced width-wise
1 lemon, zest and juice (or replace this with 8-10 drops of Young Living Essential Lemon Oil)
1 tsp. capers
1 cup chicken broth
1/4 cup flour, to coat chicken – tapioca flour is good here
2 Tbs. grape seed oil
Pinch of red pepper flakes (optional)
Sea salt and pepper to taste
Fresh basil, if available
Add fresh or frozen cauliflower or broccoli if desired

1. Slice the chicken breast. Heat pan on medium high heat, then add the 2 Tbs. grape seed oil. Heat up and add the red pepper flakes if using.

2. Add the chicken and brown on both sides. Add a little sea salt and pepper.

3. Add the chicken broth, zest of one entire lemon, and juice of the one lemon, and the capers. Let this cook until it reduces down by about half.

4. If I have fresh basil, I add it now, just before you serve it.

With this I enjoy some brown or basmati rice, or you can serve it with linguine. Add a sliced tomato or a little side salad, and you're done. Or, you can add a little broccoli or cauliflower right in the pan.

Maifun Chicken Salad for One

This is wonderful! I think the recipe is actually on the back of the noodles, and I don't have them here, but you can compare when you pick up your noodles. Of course, this is meals for one, so we're going to use a little less of everything. Here goes.

1 chicken breast, cut into bite-sized pieces
2 Tbs. oil for frying the chicken
1 stalk celery
1/4 medium onion
About 1/4 cup slivered almonds, toasted (I put these in a dry skillet over medium heat and shake them until they're lightly toasted. You have to stay with them the whole time. Don't leave them alone or they'll burn)
About 1/2 loaf of maifun (you'll find it in the Asian section of your grocery store. It pops up like popcorn when you put it in hot oil)
Another 1/2 cup for frying the maifun noodles

1. Fry the chicken breast in hot oil, then add the celery, onion and almonds. Cook until chicken is done and then set aside.

2. Clean your skillet with paper towels and reheat. Add the last 1/2 cup of oil and heat until it's hot. You can tell the oil is ready when a piece of bread browns right away instead of just sitting there looking like your last boyfriend watching his football game.

3. Add the maifun by handfuls, drain on a paper towel and then pop all the ingredients into a big bowl and toss with sesame rice dressing on page 29.

Mediterranean Chicken

1 chicken breast, sliced width-wise
2 Tbs. grape seed oil
1/4 cup flour to dust chicken
6-10 kalamata olives, sliced
1 tsp. capers
1 red bell pepper, sliced
1 summer squash, coarsely sliced
1/2 cup fresh broccoli, chopped
Red wine to deglaze the pan, about ¼ cup (you can also use lemon or lime juice and a little water, or chicken broth)
Sea salt and pepper to taste

1. Heat skillet over medium-high heat. Add grape seed oil.

2. Lightly dust the chicken with flour and add to the hot oil, then brown on both sides. Deglaze with red wine or substitute.

3. Add remaining ingredients and season with sea salt and pepper. Cook until chicken and vegetables are done, about five to seven minutes.

Serve with Rosemary Potatoes (page 158).

Murray River Curry

1 chicken breast, sliced into large bite-sized pieces
2 Tbs. grape seed oil
1/4 cup flour for dredging chicken
1 small summer squash, sliced width wise about ¼ inch thick
1 stalk broccoli, sliced width wise about ¼ inch thick
1/2 red pepper, chopped but in rather large pieces, like in 1/8 s
1/2 small onion, sliced
1 tsp. turmeric
2 tsp. garam masala
1 Tbs. fresh ginger, chopped
1/2 - 1 tsp. Murray River Australian Flake Sea salt by SaltWorks
1 cup chicken broth
Small pinch red pepper flakes
Dusting of black pepper to taste

1. Assemble all ingredients.

2. Put the chopped squash, broccoli and red pepper in a bowl altogether and add the Murray River Flake Sea salt. This is a finishing sea salt, but it adds so much to this recipe when it has a chance to just sit with these vegetables for a few minutes. The flakes are big enough, it kind of does for these vegetable what sugar does for sliced strawberries when you make strawberry shortcake. Let the vegetables sit with the sea salt for 15-30 minutes, whatever is handy.

2. Slice the chicken breast and dust with flour – use a paper towel to save on the mess. Heat skillet on medium high heat until you can't touch it comfortably with your finger. Add the oil and heat just until warm.

3. Add the turmeric, garam masala and fresh ginger. Let the spices "warm" in the oil for maybe thirty seconds or so and then add the sliced onion. Let the onion sweat a little, for maybe about a minute, then add the red pepper flakes.

4. Add the chicken. Add the black pepper.

5. Brown the chicken on both sides, then immediately add the chicken broth, then add the vegetables.

6. Keep the heat on medium high and allow the chicken broth to reduce before touching the skillet. Give it about three to five minutes, just enough time to give the chicken a chance to cook through, and then mix the vegetables into the curry so they're nicely coated.

7. Finish with a touch of Murray River sea salt.

You can add more red pepper flakes if you want more heat. I serve this with either jasmine or basmati rice and mango chutney or Cranberry Raisin Chutney (page 47).

Murray River Mediterranean Chicken

This is a similar preparation to the curry recipe on the previous page. This serves one, or two smaller eaters. Increase the recipe as needed for more diners. It is SUPER SIMPLE, and extremely tasty.

1 red pepper, sliced into large chunks
1 cup eggplant, peeled and sliced into large chunks
1 onion, sliced into large chunks
10 kalamata olives, sliced into thirds
About 1/2-1 tsp. Murray River Australian flake sea salt by Artisan Sea salt Company
2 Tbs. grape seed oil
Pinch of red pepper flakes
1 chicken breast
1/4 cup flour
Himalayan Pink Mineral Sea salt by Artisan Sea salt Company – fine

1. Toss the vegetables in a bowl with the Murray River flake Sea salt and mix them up. This is going to act a little like sugar does when you put it on strawberries. Stir occasionally while you brown the chicken.

2. Slice the chicken breast into about half inch thick pieces and dredge lightly in the flour. I put the flour on a paper towel first so I can just toss it in the garbage when I'm done.

3. Heat a skillet over medium high heat until you can't keep your finger on it, then add the oil and let it warm just a tiny bit, then add the red pepper flakes, and then add the chicken.

4. Brown the chicken on both sides, toss a little of the fine Himalayan pink sea salt and some pepper to your taste, and then add the vegetables. Don't touch anything just yet.

5. Let the chicken finish cooking, about another 5 minutes. The liquid from the vegetables will kind of steam your vegetables,

and then the last thing you'll want to do is mix it up enough to coat everything with the nummy juices that have now combined from the chicken and the vegetables.

Quick and Easy Barbecued Chicken

I usually have this with either cornbread, and/or a little potato salad (cute guy at the deli counter), and sometimes with barbecued beans for a little taste of summer, no matter what the season.

1 chicken breast, sliced
2 Tbs. grape seed oil
Barbecue sauce of your choice, or follow the easy recipe below

1. Coat the chicken using a food brush, or spoon.

2. Heat skillet over medium high heat, add oil and heat through.

3. Add chicken and turn heat down to medium. Baste chicken with the barbecue sauce, and keep turning and basting chicken until the chicken is done. This takes about ten minutes. Try not to overcook.

Quick and Easy Barbecue Sauce

1/4 Cup catsup
1 Tsp. Worcestershire sauce or Bragg's Liquid Aminos
1 Tbs. tamari
1 Tsp. sugar.

Mix ingredients together.

Quick and Easy Lemon Baked Chicken

1 chicken breast
3 Tbs. dried parsley
1 Tbs. dried basil
juice of 1/2 lemon
2 Tbs. grape seed or olive oil

1. Preheat oven to 350° while you prepare the chicken.

2. Coat chicken and bottom of oven-safe dish with the oil

3. Sprinkle on the parsley and basil, and bake at 350° for 20 minutes.

4. Remove from oven and douse with the lemon juice while the chicken is hot.

Fish, Shellfish, and Mollusk Entrees

Baked Salmon with Lemon and Capers
Chinese Style Tuna Casserole for One
Fried Oysters with Ground Millet Coating
Lemony Pancakes with Grilled Shrimp
Linguine with Clams
Mussels and Chips
Poached Salmon with Lemon
Steamed Clams with French Bread
Swordfish with Mango Salsa
Tilapia in Panko Crust

Baked Salmon with Lemon and Capers

1 salmon filet
2 Tbs. grape seed oil or butter for baking
1 tsp. capers
1/2 lemon, sliced width-wise
Extra-virgin olive oil
Sea salt and pepper to taste

1. Coat salmon with grape seed oil or butter, very lightly dust with sea salt and pepper, add capers, and bake salmon in oven proof dish at 350° for 15-20 minutes.

2. Remove salmon from oven, drizzle a little olive oil over it, add some sea salt (I like either Yakima Applewood Smoked Sea Sea salt with this one, or Snowflake®--Pacific Northwest Sea Sea salt) and freshly ground pepper, and serve.

Chinese Style Tuna Casserole for One

You can make your own wheat-free crunchy Chinese noodles. Try the recipe from Food.com posted by AzMelody on March 8, 2006. It's pretty simple and quick.

1 can tuna, drained
2/3 cup frozen peas
1 stalk celery, thinly sliced
1/4 medium onion, diced
4 or 5 mushrooms, chopped
3 Tbs. Water
1 tsp. cornstarch
1 cup vegetable stock
2 Tbs. cashews
1 cup Crunchy Chinese noodles (wheat ones, from the store. Or, make your own with sweet rice flour)

1. Mix together the tuna, frozen peas, celery, onion and mushrooms in a bowl. Set aside.

2. Mix the water and cornstarch together and add to the vegetable stock. Add this to the tuna mixture.

3. Add the cashews and the noodles.

4. Grease a loaf pan with grape seed oil. Mix together your ingredients sitting with the tuna and put it in the greased loaf pan.

5. Bake at 350° for 45 minutes. Check it after 35 minutes. It's ready when it starts to brown on the top.

I like to make this the night before, or when I come home from work, and then let it back while I change clothes and get my stretching in.

Fried Oysters with Ground Millet Coating

Here is another quick recipe for something different, and – you guessed it! You can add chips with a quick stop at McDonald's, or other chain of your choosing. Or, you can fry your own. It's just something I don't find fun to do.

12 medium oysters
1 egg plus 1 Tbs. water
1/4 cup millet flour
2 Tbs. coconut oil
Artisan Sea salt Company Alaea Sea Sea salt and pepper to taste
Lemon, if desired

1. Rinse oysters well and drain in colander.

2. Mix the egg and water. Get your flour ready on a paper towel so you can easily toss it in the garbage when you're done. Heat a cast iron skillet over medium heat. Add coconut oil.

3. Dredge the oysters, one at a time, through the flour first, then through the egg mixture, then through the flour again. Cook on one side until browned; turn over. Add sea salt and pepper. Cook second side until browned.

4. Remove to serving plate.

Ooh! Nummy. Add lemon juice, or cocktail sauce (3 Tbs. catsup, 1/8 tsp. Worcestershire Sauce, 1/4 tsp. horseradish, 1/2 tsp. turbinado sugar. Let it sit for 5 or 10 minutes for the sugar to dissolve), or tartar sauce (3 Tbs. mayonnaise, 1 Tbs. sweet or dill relish, a pinch of dried dill if you have it on hand and a squirt of lemon juice).

Lemony Pancakes with Grilled Shrimp and Lemon Sauce

2 egg whites plus 1 egg yolk (the 2nd egg yolk will be used in the lemon sauce; directions below)
1 tsp. turbinado sugar
8 drops Young Living Essential Oil Lemon Oil
1/2 tsp. baking powder
1/2 tsp. baking soda
1/8 tsp. sea salt
1/2 cup mineral water
1/2 cup gluten-free pancake mix
3 Tbs. grape seed for frying

1. Separate the egg yolks from the whites. Place the egg whites in a copper or other bowl to whip. Place one egg yolk in a small saucepan to be used for the Lemon Sauce. Place the 2nd egg yolk, sugar, lemon oil, mineral water and pancake mix in a food processor and process for about 1 minute.

2. Beat the egg whites until stiff peaks form. Fold this into the original pancake mixture you've processed and put it in the refrigerator while you make the basting sauce for the shrimp and the lemon sauce. Set these aside.

3. Remove the pancake batter from the refrigerator and fry on medium heat for about 2 minutes per side and serve, topped with the grilled shrimp and lemon sauce whose recipes follow. Preheat the broiler.

For the Grilled Shrimp

3-4 ounces raw shrimp

Basting sauce made with either equal parts commercial barbecue sauce and water, or 2 Tbs. catsup, 3 tsp. brown sugar, a dash of Worcestershire sauce, a dash of sea salt, and 1 Tbs. water. Cook in a small saucepan over medium heat until the mixture thickens up a little and set aside. You're going to brush it over the shrimp. Lightly grease a baking pan and put the shrimp under the broiler just until pink and cooked through. Serve with the lemony pancakes.

For the Lemon Sauce

1/4 cup sugar
1 tsp. cornstarch
1 drop lemon oil (or 1-1/2 Tbs. lemon juice)
1 egg yolk
1/2 cup water

Combine all ingredients in a small saucepan and cook, stirring often, until thickened. Pour over the pancakes before serving.

Linguine with Clams

1 can Snow or other quality brand chopped clams, with the juice
2 Tbs. olive oil
Pinch of red pepper flakes
1 clove garlic
1 Tbs. parsley
Sea salt and white or black pepper to taste
Linguine

1. Make linguine according to package directions for just one serving, which is a stack about the size of a quarter.

2. For the clams, heat your pan on medium heat. Add the olive oil, then the red pepper flakes, the parsley, and the garlic. Watch it carefully because these get over done really fast.

3. As soon as the garlic is a little translucent, add your clams—with the juice. Allow this to cook for about three minutes. Toss with the cooked linguine. Enjoy.

Mussels and Chips

There Is a Belgian chain restaurant that serves these and they make them wonderfully. These are very popular in France, which is where I had them for the first time.

1 lb. mussels, cleaned and the beards removed
Dry white wine or water, enough to give you at least an inch of liquid
French fries from McDonalds. Seriously, I think they have the crispiest, more wonderful French fries. I often ask them to cook them twice. They will. Go to McDonalds. Don't even try to make fries like that at home. Life is too short.

1. Cook the mussels in the white wine or water until they all open. Remove from heat.

2. Serve with the French fries. You can keep the fries warm in the oven while you make the mussels.

Tons of things could accompany this. You could do nothing and just enjoy the mussels and chips. Or, you could add some cooked greens as a side dish. Or, a simple salad. You could enjoy a soup beforehand.

Poached Salmon with Lemon and Capers

1 salmon filet (again, I keep those Costco filets on hand because they're so ... yes, handy. They're individually packed and it's easy for me to just take one out of the freezer in the morning and thaw it in the refrigerator until I get home in the evening.)
1 lemon, zest and juice
1 tsp. capers
Water
Sea salt to taste

1. In some kind of saucepan with a cover, add the salmon filet and enough water to just barely cover the top.

2. Add the lemon zest, the capers, and a pinch of sea salt. Put the lid on, heat on high heat just until boiling and then turn your heat down to medium. Cook for precisely 11 minutes and then immediately remove from heat.

3. Take the capers and lemon zest from the pan and pour over the salmon along with the lemon juice.

Ideas for side dishes: a simple salad with maybe some kind of creamy dressing (I am an absolute sucker for blue cheese dressing), or some crispy romaine with Cardini's Caesar Dressing. Broccoli would be good, too, especially steamed in the same juice as the salmon.

Steamed Clams with French Bread

1 lb. clams
Water to barely cover

This is one of those meals we don't always consider. It's so easy. If you need to clean your clams, do so by brushing the shells with a vegetable brush, then soak them for about 20 minutes in water to cover, along with about 1/2 cup sea salt to purge any sand. Dump the water and add more, to cover, and let soak for another 20 minutes. Dump that water. Now you're ready to steam the clams.

Some people use white wine, others water, or half and half. If you have a pan with a see-through lid, then you can use the lid and use less water—just about 1/2" or so. If your pan doesn't have a see-through lid, just put barely enough water to cover the clams. Bring water to a boil over high heat and watch your clams. The most important thing is to take them off the heat as soon as they open. If you have any clams that don't open, toss them out.

As for the French bread, there are several recipes online for Gluten-free French bread if you want to actually make it yourself. I use a recipe by GlutenFreeGirl. I found it at Food.com. It was published August 2, 2006. I make a batch and put the loaves in the freezer to bake when I want. Of course, if you can do some wheat, or have no problem with gluten, that's great.

Clams and a cold crisp sauvignon blanc or pinot grigio and I am transported into the heavens—no matter what the earlier part of the day was like.

Swordfish with Mango Salsa

1 swordfish steak
2-3 Tbs. coconut oil

For the Mango Salsa

Juice of one lime
1 mango, cut into bite sized pieces
3 Tbs. cucumber, diced
1/2 red onion
2 Tbs. cilantro
1 tsp. turbinado sugar
Sea salt and pepper to taste

1. Put the lime, the mango, red onion, cilantro, cucumber, sugar, sea salt and pepper in a bowl. Mix it up and let it sit for about 20 minutes.

2. Cook the swordfish on both sides in the coconut oil. Remove from pan and put it on the serving plate. Put the cilantro mixture on the plate beside it.

Enjoy! You are going to REALLY like these flavors!

Tilapia in Panko Crust

1 tilapia filet (once again, I buy mine at Costco where they're perfectly packaged and I can defrost it in the freezer during the day while I'm working.)
2 Tbs. coconut oil
3 Tbs. panko breading
3 Tbs. millet flour (I buy millet in the bulk foods section and grind it to flour in the spice grinder)
Sea salt and pepper to taste
Juice of one lemon

1. Heat pan on medium high heat. Turn heat to medium and add coconut oil.

2. Dredge tilapia filet in the Panko breading mixture (again, I use a paper towel for both the flour and the panko breading and toss the rest when I'm done.) and cook about four minutes on each side.

3. Add lemon juice and serve.

Basmati rice is a nice side, or green beans in balsamic, or just a slice tomato, or sliced beet and carrot salad.

Pork Entrees

Larsson Hash
Pork Chop with Cranberry Raisin Chutney
Pork Chow Mein
Pork Lo Mein
Pork Roast with Mint Rub
Pork Wrap
Simple Pork Ribs

Larsson Hash

This is a leftovers dish. You can make it from scratch, but why? Well, unless of course you're just in the mood for it. Or, maybe you got lucky last night and want to fix him or her breakfast before saying adios. This recipe is equally good for breakfast, lunch, or dinner. Poach an egg on the top if you like.

1 hot dog, diced
Left over beef, and / or pork and / or chicken, or a combination of two or three of these, diced
2 Tbs. Worcestershire sauce
1/2 onion, diced
1 potato, diced
2 Tbs. grape seed oil

1. Heat cast iron skillet over medium high heat until you can't touch the center with your finger.

2. Add the grape seed oil; allow to warm for a few seconds, and then add the onion and the potato until browned.

3. Add the hot dog and your meats, and allow everything to warm up. Turn your heat down to medium

4. Once you have a nice brown on your potato and onion, deglaze your pan with the Worcestershire sauce. You may need to add a little water, depending on how your stove heats. Keep stirring everything together to make sure the Worcestershire sauce is evenly distributed. Add Himalayan sea salt and freshly ground pepper to taste. Stir that in, and serve.

You can serve this alone, or top it with an egg or eggs if you're stretching it for two. You can serve lingonberry preserves if it's for lunch or dinner, and/or some sliced homemade pickled beets.

Pork Chop with Cranberry Raisin Chutney

1 pork chop
1 Tbs. grape seed oil
1 tsp. dried parsley
Sea salt and pepper

1. Rub pork chop on both sides with sea salt, pepper, and parsley.

2. Heat a small skillet on medium high heat; add the grape seed oil, and then the pork chop.

3. Sear the pork chop on both sides, then turn heat down to medium and cover the pan. Time exactly 4 minutes on each side and remove from heat.

Remove pork chop to serving plate and keep warm.

Cranberry Raisin Chutney

1 Tbs. Balsamic vinegar
1 small pinch red pepper flakes or to suit your taste
1/4 tsp. Cumin
1/8 tsp. Turmeric
1 tsp. turbinado sugar
1 Tbs. Dried cranberries
1/2 Fresh apple
A few slices of red onion, maybe 1/4 of the usual fairly large ones, finely diced

1. Deglaze the pan you cooked the pork chop in with the balsamic vinegar and scrape up the pan juices if you like.

2. Add the red pepper flakes, cumin and turmeric and let the spices develop for maybe 30 seconds.

3. Add the sugar, stirring constantly. Add the cranberries, apple and red onion. Let these cook a little over medium heat and serve with your pork chop.

You can also make this little chutney ahead of time in larger batches and keep it in the refrigerator. If doing that, increase your balsamic vinegar to 2 Tbs. and it should keep in the refrigerator for two to three weeks.

Sides: may I suggest brown basmati rice with this dish? Or, a side of cooked greens? Or, a leftover boiled potato, halved or quartered, cooked alongside the pork chop?

Pork Chow Mein

This is one of those dishes that is made very easily from the pork roast with mint rub; or, you can do it from scratch too.

4 ounce cooked pork, cut shoestring or julienne style
A handful of fresh bean sprouts
1 Tbs. grape seed oil
Small pinch red pepper flakes, if desired
2 stalks celery, thinly sliced
2 green onions, sliced
1/2 can water chestnuts—or, you can use a full can, especially if you like them
A few mushrooms, if desired
Chow mein noodles (I like to use the crispy ones because I love crispy things)
1/2 cup chicken or vegetable stock
Slurry made with 1 tsp. cornstarch and 4 Tbs. water
1 Tbs. Tamari
Toasted sesame seeds

1. Have the cut pork ready, in a large bowl, off to the side, along with the bean sprouts and water chestnuts.

2. Heat a wok or skillet over medium high heat; add the oil, then the vegetables. I've found that you get a better blend of vegetables if you cook them individually. Once cooked, add them to a bowl where you have your cooked pork waiting.

3. Once everything has been cooked, over medium heat, add the chicken or vegetable stock and get it nice and bubbly.

4. Add the tamari and the cornstarch slurry, and then add the pork and the vegetables. Keep everything moving, tossing to coat with the tamari mixture, until everything is heated through.

5. Garnish with some toasted sesame seeds and additional tamari to suit your taste.

If you haven't explored using chop sticks yet, you might want to do that now. I think it's probably a great anti-Alzheimer's activity.

Pork Lo Mein

If you have a chance to make homemade soba noodles sometime, do so. You can get the whole recipe from the internet by looking up Homemade Buckwheat Soba Noodles. It was posted by Kimi Harris on May 19, 2009, under the Nourishing Gourmet. That recipe makes 6 servings and they freeze pretty well. It's gluten-free because, as you know already I think, buckwheat is not wheat. I have a pasta maker attachment to my Kitchen Aide mixer that I love. These homemade ones taste twice as good as the soba noodles you buy in the store. But, if that's what's available, no worries, the dish will still be satisfying—and quick.

4 ounce cooked or barbecued pork, cut julienne or shoestring style
1 Tbs. sesame oil
Pinch red pepper flakes, if desired
2 cups (approximately) Chinese cabbage, sliced
1 Carrot, thinly sliced
1/3 medium onion, thinly sliced
Homemade soba noodles

1. Cook the soba noodles and have them ready.

2. Heat the wok or skillet over medium high heat. Cook, separately, the cabbage, the carrot and the onion. Put them in the bowl with the pork and toss them all together. Serve with the soba noodles and enjoy, enjoy, enjoy.

Pork Roast with Mint Rub

I buy pork roasts from Costco in a package of three. They last me for one meal as is, plus one or two pork sandwiches, and a fried rice or fettuccini dish with the rest

1 tiny pork roast, the smallest you can find
2 Tbs. olive oil, grape seed oil or canola oil
2 Tbs. dry mint leaves
2 Tbs. dried parsley
1 tsp. dried basil
½ tsp. pepper
½ tsp. sea salt

1. Coat roast with oil and rub on the seasoning and spices.

2. Bake in a 325 degree oven for one hour and forty minutes.

What a treat this is! You can add a potato, carrot and onion, or you can take it the other way and maybe have some gnocchi as a side dish.

Pork Wrap

4 ounce Left over pork, cut matchstick style
Cellophane noodles, about 1/4 of a package
1/4 – 1/2 cucumber, depending on size and type, cut into matchsticks
1 Carrot, peeled and cut into matchsticks (par-boiled if you prefer)
Fresh mint leaves
Fresh cilantro leaves
4 Rice paper wrappers
Spicy chili sauce
1/4 red pepper, sliced into matchsticks
Peanut sauce (to follow)

1. Toss the carrot into a hot water bath just long enough to soften them up a bit. You can cook the cellophane noodles in the same water. And, when you take out the cellophane noodles, you can soak the rice paper wrapper in the same water for a few seconds to soften. Set aside.

2. Place the rice paper wrappers on parchment paper or a sushi board. Fill with matchstick slices of pork, cellophane noodles, carrots, cucumber, and red pepper.

3. Put a small amount of peanut sauce over the top of the veggies. Roll up the wrappers nice and tight by folding the ends in and then rolling them up.

Serve this with peanut sauce and sweet chili sauce, mixed together.

Peanut sauce

1/4 cup peanut butter, creamy or crunchy—your call
1/4 cup water
1 Tbs. lime juice
1/4 tsp. ground cumin
1/4 tsp. ground coriander

Dash sea salt
Small pinch red pepper flakes, if desired
1 clove garlic, minced, if desired

Warm all ingredients together over medium heat, stirring constantly to mix ingredients, until mixture is warm and smooth. Use this to dip your wraps in. If you have any leftovers (unlike me) they'll keep in the refrigerator for a few days, or you can put them in the freezer for a month or so.
If you have some extra peanuts lying about, especially those wonderful old fashioned blister peanuts from Trader Joe's, you can grind up a few of those in your spice grinder to drizzle over the top of your wraps.

Simple Pork Ribs

You can do this on the grill or in your oven. Grill at medium for 1-2 hours. Or, in the oven at 350° for one hour, then up to 400° for another 30 minutes.

2 or 3 pork ribs or whatever you consider being a serving, from your local butcher or grocer's meat department

1. Rub ribs all over with ground pepper and sea salt (I suggest either Yakima Applewood smoked sea sea salt, or Salish Alderwood smoked sea sea salt by Artisan Sea salt Company. Available from SaltWorks whose information appears in the references section of this cookbook)

2. Wrap loosely in two layers of aluminum foil and place in your preheated 350° oven for one hour.

3. Remove the ribs from the oven and crank up the heat to 400°.

4. Remove ribs from foil and brush on the barbecue sauce of your choice (I use a homemade combination of 3 Tbs. catsup, splash of tamari, 1 tsp. brown sugar and 1 tsp. Worcestershire sauce, warmed lightly to melt the sugar and incorporate the flavors). Leave the ribs open now and heat at 400° for 15 minutes. Turn, brush sauce on the other side and bake another 15 minutes.

A salad or cooked greens of some kind go really well with this. So does rice if you want a starch, or creamy polenta, or corn muffins.

Pasta Entrees

Artichoke Hearts, Sun Dried Tomatoes and Penne
Baked Penne with Kale
Fennel Flavored Risotto for 100
Josie Pennello's Unforgettable Spaghetti Sauce
Mac and Cheese for One
Pasta Putanesca
Pasta with Red Pepper and Peas
Pasta with Prosciutto and Peppers
Spaghetti Frittata

Artichoke Hearts, Sun-Dried Tomatoes and Penne

This is really good with sausage. I realize not everyone does sausage because of the fat content, or the cholesterol, but once in a while it's wonderful. Pick and choose your moment. Pick and choose your sausage, since there are so many available. Or, just get some plain mild Italian sausage from your butcher. If it's loose, fry it up. If it's encased, slice it and then fry it.

3 artichoke hearts, halved
2 Tbs. sun-dried tomatoes
1 serving gluten-free penne pasta
1 Tbs. grape seed oil
Pinch of red pepper flakes
1 clove garlic if desired
Grated parmesan or Romano cheese, if desired

1. Cook the penne according to manufacturer's direction, or use leftover pasta you have on hand. Drain.

2. To a cast iron pan, add the grape seed oil, red pepper flakes, and garlic if using it. Warm just until the garlic exudes its aroma. Don't let it brown.

3. Add the drained pasta, the sun dried tomatoes and the artichokes.

4. If serving this with Italian sausage, cook the sausage separately and add once the vegetables have been warmed. Top with the grated cheese, if using.

Baked Penne with Kale

This is great with a side salad and balsamic vinaigrette dressing. Or, with a side of acorn or Delicata squash.

4 ounce penne pasta
3 cups kale, washed, ribs removed, sliced into ribbons
1/4 red onion, finely chopped
2 Tbs. tomato paste (this is easy if you open a can of tomato paste, both ends, and push out the tomato paste into a plastic sandwich bag. Use what you need and freeze the rest. It will be easy to measure and use next time too.)
1 – 12 ounce can tomatoes
1 cup grated Parmigiano-Reggiano or pecorino Romano cheese

1. Cook the pasta according to manufacturer's direction.

2. Toss in the onion and the kale while the pasta is cooking for the last 5 minutes. Drain.

3. Chop the tomatoes inside the can, and then add them to the pan along with the tomato paste.

4. Stir over low to medium heat until the tomato paste warms up, breaks down and envelopes the other ingredients.

5. Add the cheese and put this in an oven-safe dish. Bake at 350° for thirty minutes and serve.

Josie Pennello's Unforgettable Spaghetti Sauce

My son's grandmother taught me how to make this recipe. Yes, it makes more than one serving, but, really, how bad is it to have leftover spaghetti that you just have to heat up? I suppose you could freeze the rest, but I've always eaten it before it spoiled—well before. This is how I remember it, and how I've been making it these last almost forty years. Too much spaghetti, I think, is a little like leftover wine--huh??? It doesn't exist in my house.

2 Tbs. olive oil
1 pinch red pepper flakes
2 cloves garlic (or as many as you like personally; even if you leave it out of this dish entirely, it's still divine)
¼ cup fresh parsley when available; or 2 Tbs. dried parsley
1 lb. extremely lean hamburger
1 onion, chopped
1 can tomato paste, plus two cans water
1-21 ounce can whole tomatoes, plus one can water
2 Tbs. sugar
Sea salt and pepper to taste

1. Heat a large saucepan over medium heat; add the olive oil, red pepper flakes, garlic and parsley. Heat just until the garlic becomes translucent (don't let it brown), and then immediately add the onion.

2. Cook until the onion has sweated and becomes nearly translucent. Add the hamburger and sea salt lightly. Cook until browned.

3. Add the can of tomato paste and mix it in, allowing the paste to melt in the pan. Add 1 can of water to clean the spoon, and a second can of water to clean the can.

4. Add the whole tomatoes. I like to put mine through a food mill to take out the seeds and the peels, but you can cut them

inside the can and just put them in as is if you like. Add 1 can of water. Give it a good stir now, and then add the sugar to the top. FROM THIS MOMENT UNTIL YOUR SAUCE STARTS TO BUBBLE, DO NOT TOUCH IT.

5. Once the sauce has come to a good boil, then you can stir it, paying special attention to get around the edges and the bottom. Turn it down to low or medium low so you keep a nice little boil on it and allow it to just sit there and boil for several hours.

I like to put my sauce on in the morning, on a Saturday, say, and let it cook all day long. Adjust your heat to the time you have available to hang out and keep an eye on it; or, at this point you could put it into a pre-heated slow cooker I suppose and let it cook unattended all day long. You can make a more intense broth by getting pork neck bones from your butcher, boiling them down, taking the useable meat and retaining the liquid. Separate the liquid and let it sit for 24 hours in the refrigerator. Remove the fat that coagulates. What's left is food fit for the gods. Either way you want to make it, fast or slow, it's magnificent.

Remember the freshly grated parmesan or Romano cheese for the top.

Mac and Cheese for One

4 ounce dry elbow macaroni
3/4 cup grated non-dairy, or regular cheddar, cheese
1/4 onion, finely diced
3 Tbs. extra virgin olive oil
Sea salt and pepper to taste

1. Boil the macaroni using the manufacturer's recommendations and your personal preference. I like mine al dente. It's usually about 5 - 7 minutes.

2. Drain the pasta in a colander, draining nearly all of the water, but not all entirely. I usually leave about 3 Tbs. of water still in the pan.

3. After you drain the pasta, return the pan to medium heat and add the onion. Cook until the onion is translucent. Since it's diced so finely, this doesn't take long and the little water left in the pan is usually enough. If not, add a little more water to the pan.

4. Once the onion is done, return the macaroni to the pan, turn off the heat, add the cheese, stir until the cheese is melted and blended in, then add the olive oil and sea salt and pepper to taste.

5. Toss everything until all the pasta is nicely coated. Serve.

This is tasty with a small salad served with thinly sliced cucumber and cooked beets, tossed with red wine vinaigrette.

Pasta Putanesca

This is a great recipe for the time when the tomatoes are their freshest and juiciest. I adapted this from Delia Smith's Summer Cookbook. If you're not a huge anchovy fan, you can cut down on those to half a can, but I have to tell you they melt right in and the only thing you'll notice is the really wonderful depth of flavor. It's important to use a really good quality anchovy here, a name you know and trust. I made this once with an off brand and I was very disappointed.

1/2 - 1 can anchovies, drained (depending on how much you like anchovies)
1 Tbs. tomato paste
1/2 lb. fresh tomatoes, skinned, seeded, and chopped
3/4 cup kalamata olives, finely chopped
Pinch of red pepper flakes
1/4 Cup chopped fresh basil, if available (you can substitute 1 Tbs. dried basil if mandatory)

1. Heat the oil in a medium saucepan over medium high heat. Add the red pepper flakes, then the basil--if using dried. If using fresh basil, save it for last. Heat just to you can smell their aroma, and then add the other ingredients.

2. Turn the heat to low and simmer the sauce very gently without a lid for about forty minutes. It's going to turn into a lovely thick mass. Top with fresh basil.

I like to serve this with linguine, and a nice bold Italian red wine. I'm generally too sated to add a salad or anything, but I suppose you could. I would have the salad, though, at the end of the meal.

Pasta with Red Pepper and Peas

Again, this is good with leftover pasta. You can make the pasta just for this one meal, but leftover is wonderful too.

1 cup Frozen peas
1/4 red bell pepper, diced
1 Tbs. sun dried tomatoes, if desired
1/4 medium onion, thinly sliced
Leftover pasta (any kind of pasta is fine. I prefer penne, spaghetti, linguine or fettuccine)
1/4 cup water
1 Tbs. extra virgin olive oil
Parmigiano-Reggiano or pecorino Romano cheese, if you can do aged cheeses, grated

1. Add the pasta and water to a warm skillet along with the red bell pepper, the tomatoes if using, and the onion. Cover. Cook just until warmed, about 5-7 minutes over medium heat.

2. Uncover. Add the frozen peas. Toss.

3. Cook until the peas are warm but still bright green.

4. Remove from heat and add the olive oil, and sea salt and freshly ground pepper to taste. Add the grated cheese as desired.

Pasta with Prosciutto and Peppers

1 serving of spaghetti or your pasta of choice
2 slices prosciutto, cut into strips
2 Tbs. grape seed oil
Pinch red pepper flakes, if desired
1 clove garlic, chopped, if desired
1/4 red bell pepper, sliced
1/4 yellow bell pepper, sliced
1/4 medium red onion, thinly sliced
1 tsp. capers
Sea salt and pepper to taste
Parmigiano-Reggiano or pecorino Romano cheese, grated, if desired
1 Tbs. extra virgin olive oil
Fresh basil if available

1. Warm a small skillet over medium / medium high heat until it's too hot to touch with your finger. Add the grape seed oil, allow it to warm, and then add the red pepper flakes and the garlic. Almost immediately (don't let the garlic get brown), add the prosciutto and cook until it's crispy.

2. Add the peppers and the onion and cook until the vegetables are just cooked through. Add the capers.

3. Remove from heat. Toss with the cooked pasta and the olive oil. Add sea salt and pepper to taste. Add fresh basil if available. Add the grated cheese if desired.

Spaghetti Frittata

Inspired by Nick Stellino's pasta frittata, this is a really handy recipe for using leftover pasta (what? You might ask. You may have already used that up along with the leftover wine...or, not...)

Leftover spaghetti, about 1/2 cup
2 Tbs. butter or grape seed oil for frying
Several leaves of fresh basil, chopped
Parmigiano-Reggiano or pecorino roman cheese, grated
3 Tbs. water
1 or 2 eggs, depending on how hungry you are and what's on hand
Pinch of red pepper flakes

1. Chiffonade the basil and set aside. Mix the egg, or eggs, with the water and set aside.

2. Using a small skillet, heat it over medium high heat until you can't touch the center with your finger. Add 2 Tbs. butter and let it melt until brown. Add the red pepper flakes.

3. Add the spaghetti, tossing the spaghetti until it's just warmed through. It's okay if it gets a little crunchy on the bottom. In fact, some people like that best.

4. Preheat the broiler.

5. Pour the egg mixture over the spaghetti. Use a fork like you would with a regular omelet, kind of poking through the mixture to the bottom of the skillet to get a good deal of the egg cooked.

6. Once the eggs are pretty much set, and it looks like the bottom is getting brown, put it under the broiler to finish cooking the last of the egg. Pull it from the broiler and set it on a cool surface. Especially if you're not using a non-stick skillet,

this will enable the skillet to unlock your frittata for you. Add the basil, sea salt and pepper, and the grated cheese. Serve.

This is heavenly for any meal, but I usually use it for breakfast, brunch or lunch.

Vegetarian Entrees

Beet Green Frittata
Egg Foo Young for One
Gluten-Free Cornmeal-Based Pizza Dough
I have Too Many Greens This Week Pie
Metropolitan Pizza
Tofu Omelet
Vege Sushi roll
Vegetable Coconut Curry with Egg
Zucchini Parmesan with Tomato Sauce

Beet Green Frittata

This makes a nice lunch, a hearty breakfast, or a lovely light dinner.

1 Tbs. butter
2 eggs
2 Tbs. water
About two cups fresh beet greens, rinsed and chopped
1 pinch red pepper flakes
1/4 small onion, or more if desired, finely chopped

1. Beat the 2 eggs with the water and set aside.

2. Heat skillet over medium high heat until you can't leave your finger in the center. Add butter. Add the red pepper flakes, then the onion and beet greens.

3. Cook the beet greens until done, until they've wilted and become that beautiful dark green color.

4. Add your eggs and use a fork or spatula in a rather rapid motion in small shoves away from you so that the eggs begin to cook fairly evenly. Preheat the broiler. Remove the pan from the heat and put under the broiler just until done. You want to watch this closely so the eggs don't dry out.

5. Put the skillet on a cool surface to more easily release the frittata. Serve.

Add some freshly grated parmesan or Romano cheese, and maybe a sliced tomato on the side.

Egg Foo Young for One

2 Tbs. grape seed oil
1 clove garlic, if desired
1/4 cup Napa cabbage
1/4 cup fresh bean sprouts
1 green onion, chopped
1 Tbs. cilantro, if desired, chopped
1 Tbs. tamari
1/8 tsp. sugar
1 egg plus 1 tsp. water, well beaten
1 tsp. sesame oil
1/8 tsp. sea salt (I choose Celtic sea sea salt)
1 more Tbs. grape seed oil
Brown sauce (recipe follows)
Toasted sesame seeds and another sliced green onion, if desired

1. Heat wok or skillet over high heat. Add the grape seed oil and swirl to coat pan.

2. Add garlic and toss until fragrant but not browned.

3. Add Napa cabbage, bean sprouts and green onion and toss well.

4. Add cilantro (if using), tamari, and sugar, and cook, tossing often, until cabbage is just tender, 1 or 2 minutes.

5. Transfer to plate and spread it out in a single layer to allow this mixture to cool.

Meanwhile, combine egg, sesame oil, sea salt and the Napa cabbage mixture and blend well. Heat wok or small skillet over high heat, and add the egg mixture. Keep this mixture swirling to cook the egg and then flip it over for a few seconds. Remove from heat and keep warm, if using brown sauce. Otherwise, serve now.

Brown Sauce

1/4 cup water
1 Tbs. tamari
1/8 tsp. sugar
1 tsp. cornstarch, dissolved in 3 Tbs. water
1/4 tsp. sesame oil

Put ingredients in a small saucepan and cook over medium heat. Bring to a boil, boil until the sugar is dissolved, watching constantly, and then add your cornstarch slurry. Cook just until the mixture thickens and remove from heat. Top your omelet and toss on another green onion, sliced, and some toasted sesame seeds if you like.

Gluten-Free Pizza Dough

This recipe was adapted from *Gluten-Free Baking for Dummies* I found on the internet. Cornmeal adds crunch to this simple crust. Plus, you don't need to wait for the dough to rise so it's super quick. This makes one 10" crust.

3/4 cup cornmeal
1/3 cup sweet rice flour
1/3 cup millet flour
1/3 cup potato flour
3 Tbs. buckwheat flour
2 Tbs. extra virgin olive oil
1-1/2 tsp. baking powder
1/2 tsp. baking soda
1/2 tsp. sea salt (for a bit of a smoky flavor, try Salish Alder Smoked sea salt/fine (manufactured by Artisan Sea salt Company and available at SaltWorks.com)
1 cup mineral water
Your choice of toppings

1. Preheat oven to 425°.

2. Put the flours together in the bowl of your stand-up mixer and blend on low using the whisk attachment until you have only one color.

3. Switch to the dough attachment and add the remaining ingredients. Beat for 2 minutes.

4. Put a little coconut or grape seed oil on a pizza pan, dust with more cornmeal, and spread the pizza dough thinly.

5. Bake at 425° for 15 minutes. Remove from the oven. Add your toppings. Bake another 10-15 minutes until your pizza is nicely browned. Allow the pizza to cool on a wire rack for just a minute or so before slicing for best results.

I Have Too Many Greens This Week Pie

Sometimes even those green vegetable bags don't keep greens heavenly for as long as we might like. When that happens, I make this recipe. It's simple. And, it's very tasty. If I have a guest over, I add a top crust and brush it with a little egg wash (egg combined with a teaspoon of water).

Bottom crust for one 8 inch pie
Greens of your choice, about 6 cups, chopped (these should be washed and stems removed. You can use a combination of mustard greens, swiss chard, kale, beet greens—any kind of greens you have on hand)
1/4 cup water
1/2 medium onion or 2 shallots, chopped
4 or 5 mushrooms, chopped
1/4 tsp. turbinado sugar
1/4 cup Parmigiano-Reggiano cheese or pecorino Romano, grated
1/4 cup finely chopped toasted walnuts (optional)

1. Preheat oven to 350°.

2. Put your greens in a large skillet with a tight fitting lid and the 1/4 cup of water. Start the pan on medium high heat and as soon as the water boils, turn to medium heat and keep the lid on. Cook over medium heat for about 4 minutes, depending on your stove. Remove lid. Set aside.

3. Make your bottom crust and have it ready in your pie pan.

4. Over medium heat in a medium sized skillet, add the onion or shallot. Put the lid on for 2 minutes to soften them. Add the turbinado sugar.

5. Reduce heat to medium low and cook, stirring occasionally, for 15 minutes.

6. Add the mushrooms. Cook together another 5 minutes. Add to the greens mixture.

7. Add the grated cheese. Mix everything together really well to make sure the cheese is distributed. Fill the pie pan. Sprinkle the walnuts, if using, over the top.

8. Bake in a 350° oven for 40 minutes or until the crust has browned.

Metropolitan Pizza

I've included a gluten-free pizza crust recipe in this section, or you can use one of your own G-F recipes, or a premade pizza crust from Trader Joe's, or your local bakery. If you are not a vegetarian, you can add prosciutto, sliced width-wise into about 1/4 inch or 1/2 inch strips, for a nice touch.

1 Pizza crust
2 Tbs. coconut oil
About 2 Tbs. Sun dried tomatoes, chopped
About 1/2 cup marinated artichoke hearts, sliced
About 1/4 cup Kalamata olives, sliced

1. Roll out the pizza crust to the thickness you like.

2. Warm the coconut oil in a saucepan and brush on to the pizza crust.

3. Add the remaining ingredients and bake at 425° for 10 - 12 minutes. Remove from the oven and serve immediately. Add freshly grated parmesan cheese and red pepper flakes if desired.

Tofu Omelet

This recipe was adapted from the book Eat Right For Your Blood type by Dr. peter J. D'Adamo with Catherine Whitney.

1 egg
4 ounce (1/4 container) firm tofu
1/4 tsp. turmeric
2 tsp. tamari
1 Tbs. grape seed or canola oil

1. Stir the egg, tofu, turmeric and tamari together in a bowl.

2. Heat a small frying pan over medium heat until your finger can't touch it comfortably. Add the oil, swirl it around, and then dump out any excess. Who needs the extra fat and calories, right? Or, you could use a cooking spray if you prefer. You just need the pan lightly coated.

3. Add the egg mixture to the pan, put a lid on it and cook for 10 minutes over medium heat.

4. After 10 minutes, take the pan off the heat and let stand on a cool surface for 2 minutes. This allows the last of the cooking to take place, plus it allows the skillet to slightly cool, enabling your omelet to come out of the pan easily. Serve.

Vege Sushi Rolls

Cut the following into matchsticks:
1 carrot, parboiled or cooked through
1 Persian cucumber, or the equivalent amount of greenhouse or regular cucumber (take out the seeds if using a regular cucumber—you can do this with a tea spoon)
1/4 red or yellow bell pepper
3 or 4 sheets toasted nori (available at Asian markets)
1 recipe sushi rice (below)
Chinese green mustard
Tamari sauce

Sushi rice (Recipe adapted from AllRecipes.com, Perfect Sushi Rice)

1 cup uncooked glutinous white rice (sushi rice; do not use long grain rice)
1-1/2 cups water
1/4 cup rice vinegar
1/2 Tbs. vegetable oil
1/8 cup turbinado sugar
1/2 tsp. sea salt

1. In a small saucepan, combine the vinegar, the oil, the sugar and the sea salt. Cook over medium heat until the sugar dissolves. Set aside to cool.

2. Rinse the rice until the water runs clear. Put the rice in a pan with the water, put a lid on it and bring it to a boil. Reduce the heat to low and boil for 20 minutes. Remove from heat. Cool (if I'm in a hurry, I sometimes put the pan in a cold water bath up to halfway up the top of the pan).

3. Mix the wet ingredients with the rice thoroughly. It will seem very wet at first until the rice dries and absorbs it all.

4. Now—Get out your sushi mat. You can use parchment or waxed paper in a pinch I suppose, but why? Sushi mats are affordable, simple to use, and believe me, you need one.

5. Lay out a sheet of nori. Lay down some sushi rice, almost to the edge, but leave about 1/8 inch for your seal. In the middle, put a little of the vegetables, and then roll up your rolls.

Have some Chinese green mustard and tamari ready to blend a little together to dip your rolls in. Have some pickled ginger between bites to refresh your palate. A couple of umeboshi plums are very tasty alongside too.

These are fun if it's something you feel like doing, or you're in an out of the way place and feel like Japanese take-out without going out. If you have a safe provider of sushi grade fish, you can add fish to this as well. Or, have the fish on the side as sashimi.

Vegetable Coconut Curry with Egg

1 Tbs. grape seed oil
1 medium carrot, sliced into 1/2 or 1 inch chunks
1/2 - 1 cup Cauliflower and/ or green beans (depending on how hungry you are)
*1/2 cup Chick peas/garbanzo beans (retain the liquid; don't throw it out)
Patak's hot curry paste – start with 1/4 tsp. You can always add more
1/2 cup Coconut milk
1/2 medium onion, diced
1 hardboiled egg, whole
1/2 cup Basmati rice
1 cup water
Dash of sea salt

1. Heat a large skillet over medium heat. Add the grape seed oil, then the carrot, cauliflower, green beans and onion. Stir until the onions become translucent.

2. Mix the curry paste in with the coconut milk and add this to the skillet. You have to be careful with the curry paste because it's very concentrated and very spicy hot. Turn the heat down to low and let the mixture kind of bubble along. Cook for 10 minutes. While you're doing this, put on your rice.

3. Add 1/2 cup basmati rice to a small saucepan along with the cup of water and the dash of sea salt. Bring to a boil over medium high heat. Reduce to low heat and cook for 20 minutes for white basmati rice and 35-40 minutes for brown basmati rice.

4. Check your curry. You may need to add a little more coconut milk, depending on your stove, and your tastes. Taste the curry sauce now to check for flavor and heat. Adjust with either more coconut milk or curry paste as necessary. And, add your

hardboiled egg at this time. Keep this mixture on low heat for another 10 minutes, or until your rice is done.

*Note: The rest of the chick peas can be used to make hummus. Just put them in a food processor with a clove of garlic, 3 Tbs. of the chick pea liquid, 3 Tbs. lemon juice, 1/2 Tbs. Tahini and about 1 Tbs. olive oil. Process to a paste. Serve it on crackers, with crudités, or as a sandwich spread.

Zucchini Parmesan

This is a great main dish. Leftovers make a wonderful side dish or lunch. Or, you can make it the night before you're going to want it and then just warm it up. Pretend it's the Cook's night out but he's prepared something wonderful for you.

2 small or 1 medium zucchini, sliced
1/2 cup parmesan cheese, freshly grated fine
1 egg plus 2 Tbs. water, whisked together
1/2 cup brown rice flour
2 Tbs. grape seed oil for frying
Sea salt and pepper to taste
2 Tbs. extra virgin olive oil (EVOO)

Tomato Sauce

2 Tbs. tomato paste (you can cut both sides of a tomato paste can and push out the paste into a small plastic baggie. Use as much as you need at a time and freeze the rest)
1 Tbs. dried basil
1 Tbs. grape seed oil
Pinch of red pepper flakes
1 clove garlic, if desired
1-16 ounce can whole tomatoes, chopped in the can
1 tsp. sugar

1. Preheat the oven to 350°

2. Heat a cast iron skillet on medium/medium high heat and add grape seed oil.

3. Dredge zucchini in flour, then the egg, and then the flour again. Brown on both sides and set aside on paper towels to drain the oil.

4. Make the tomato sauce: start by heating a saucepan over medium heat. Add grape seed oil, and garlic if using. Add the tomato paste and stir to warm it up. Add the chopped

tomatoes. Add the sugar, sort of laying the sugar on top of the sauce; don't mix it in. Let the mixture come to a boil and do not touch it. This will remove a lot of the acid. Cook over medium / medium low heat for about 20 - 30 minutes. Stir well, especially from the sides and bottom. It's ready to use in your recipe.

5. Stack in a baking dish (I use a bread pan) coated with the 1 Tbs. of EVOO, alternating with the zucchini with the tomato sauce and the parmesan cheese.

6. Bake at 350° for 30-40 minutes, depending on your oven. Serve.

Side Dishes

Baked Fennel
Broccoli Bake
Butternut Squash Soufflé for One
Cauliflower Steaks
Fennel Flavored Risotto for 100
Fried Rice
Green Beans with Balsamic Finish
Greens Sautéed or Steamed with Onion
Hasselback Potato
Mélange of Root Vegetables with Fennel
 Mélange of Zucchini, Carrot, Beet and Onion
Oil Me Rosemary Sliced Delicata Squash
Roasted Root Vegetable with Balsamic Reduction
Rosemary Potato
Twice Baked Potato
Zesty Cauliflower
Zucchini Chips

Baked Fennel

2 Tbs. grape seed oil
1 Fresh fennel bulb
Sea salt, to taste
Freshly ground black pepper to taste
Extra virgin olive oil, if desired
Freshly grated parmesan or Romano cheese, if desired

1. Preheat oven to 350°.

2. Slice fennel bulb in half and remove the core. Slice width-wise and place on cookie sheet lightly coated with grape seed oil.

3. Bake at 350° for 20 minutes. Remove from the oven, add fresh olive oil and sea salt and pepper to taste. If desired, add freshly grated parmesan cheese.

Broccoli Bake

2 cups broccoli, chopped
3 Tbs. butter, melted
1/4 cup bread crumbs
1/4 cup grated parmesan cheese

1. Parboil the broccoli in boiling water for about 2 minutes.

2. Coat an oven safe dish with either butter, grape seed oil, coconut oil or other oil of choice.

3. Put your broccoli in the dish, sprinkle the melted butter over it, then sprinkle the bread crumbs, and then the parmesan cheese.

4. Bake uncovered at 450° for about 15 minutes.

This same recipe can be used for cauliflower florets with great success.

Butternut Squash Soufflé for One

2 tsp. grape seed oil
2 tsp. gluten-free white flour
4 ounce hot mashed squash
2 Tbs. turbinado sugar
Dash nutmeg
Dash cinnamon
Dash sea salt (I like Yakima Applewood Smoked Sea Sea salt by SaltWorks) or to taste
Freshly ground pepper to taste
1 drop vanilla
1 egg separated, plus 2 egg whites
Toasted pecans, about 2 Tbs.

1. Preheat oven to 325°.

2. In a small saucepan, melt grape seed oil over medium heat. Stir in flour and cook until bubbly, about 30 seconds. Add the toasted pecans. Remove from heat. Wait another 90 seconds and whisk in the egg yolk. Set aside.

3. Whip the egg white until stiff. Using a rubber spatula, fold the egg whites into the flour and egg yolk mixture by going under the batter and lifting up and through the batter until combined.

4. Spoon into a 10 ounce oven safe dish with straight sides, level the top, and then to run your finger around the inside rim of the dish to make a little canal around the top of the soufflé to help it to rise better. Bake in a pre-heated 325 ° oven until the soufflé is set, about 20 minutes. Serve immediately.

Cauliflower Steaks

These look pretty, and different, and the browning brings out the bit of sweetness.

1 head of cauliflower
1 Tbs. grape seed oil
Sea salt and pepper to taste

1. Beginning at the middle of the head of cauliflower, cut straight down and through, cutting it in half. Now, cut slices from the half outward until you can't cut anymore steaks and the cauliflower starts to fall apart. Use the extra cauliflower for another dish or add it to your weekly vegetable broth or soup.

2. In a large skillet (I like cast iron) warmed over medium heat, add the grape oil and warm. Add the cauliflower steaks. Cover. Brown on each side, adding sea salt and pepper after you turn them over. Depending on the kind of pan you use for this, you may need to add 2 or 3 Tbs. water, or up to 1/4 Cup, in order to get the steaks completely done without burning them, or turn your heat down.

3. Serve as is, or add a little EVOO and additional sea salt and pepper.

Fennel Flavored Risotto for 100

Okay, this isn't for a hundred. But, it's not really for one either. Even though it is for one, by the time you make risotto, you may as well make enough to enjoy over the course of a couple of meals. I make mine in the pressure cooker. Good luck to anyone who has the patience and time to cook this particular meal just on the stove top. You won't find me there. Trust me, this is a wonderful meal—and it's worth investing in a pressure cooker. This recipe is adapted from Pressure Perfect by Lorna Sass.

1 Tbs. butter
1/4 cup finely chopped onions
1-1/2 cups aborio rice
1/2 cup dry white wine or dry vermouth
3-1/2 – 4 cups chicken broth
3 – 4 drops Young Living Essential Oil Fennel oil
3 Tbs. fresh parsley, if desired

1. Heat the butter in the pressure cooker.

2. Add the onions and cook over high heat for one minute, stirring frequently.

3. Stir in the rice and make sure it gets coated with the butter.

4. Pour in the wine (carefully, since it can spatter). Cook over high heat until the rice has absorbed the wine, about 30 seconds.

5. Stir in 3-1/2 cups of broth. Lock the lid in place and bring to high pressure over high heat and cook for 4 minutes. Turn off the heat.

6. Quick-release the pressure by setting the cooker under cold running water. Remove the lid and cook over medium high head stirring vigorously. Cook uncovered, stirring every minute, until the risotto thickens. It will be tender but chewy. This takes about 5 minutes.

7. Turn off the heat and stir in the essential fennel oil and fresh parsley if using.

This is good with anything. It's especially nice with a fat sausage. Or, if you're very hungry, then, a fat sausage and some cooked mixed greens with olive oil, sea salt and pepper.

Fried Rice

This is a nice easy little meal to make whenever. It's tasty for breakfast, or anytime you have leftover rice. It's also another way to get your greens in.

Greens, about a cup, cleaned and coarsely chopped
Cooked, leftover rice
1 pinch red pepper flakes
1 pinch of parsley
1 egg, whisked with 1 tsp. water
2 Tbs. grape seed or canola oil
1 green onion, sliced
1/2 cup Frozen peas
2 tsp. Tamari

1. In a large skillet, heat the oil over medium high heat.

2. Add the parsley and the red pepper flakes, cook for just about 30 seconds, and then add the onion.

3. Add the frozen peas and the egg. Add the tamari sauce.

4. Keep the mixture moving until the eggs are just cooked and remove from heat while the peas are still a vibrant green. Serve.

Green Beans with Balsamic Finish

1 bunch fresh green beans, nipped, washed, and whole
1 small pinch red pepper flakes
1 Tbs. grape seed oil, or other oil of choice
1 Tbs. balsamic vinegar

1. Heat pan over medium heat, add the oil, then add the red pepper flakes, and then add the fresh green beans. Cover. Cook for about three to five minutes, just until they're tender, but still a nice brilliant green.

2. Remove the cover and add the balsamic vinegar. Toss to coat and remove to plate or serving platter. Add a little finishing sea salt such as Murray River Australian Flake Sea salt or Cyprus Flake Sea Sea salt.

Greens Sautéed or Steamed with Onion

I watched some program with Rachel Ray once and she said the onion took away the bitterness of the greens. I've been using onion for that purpose ever since, and it seems to work. Thank you, Rachel.

3 cups greens (any combination, or all the same. You might use kale, beet greens, chard, or turnip greens--or, a combination of all of these)
1/4 medium onion
1/4 cup water
Extra virgin olive oil
Sea salt and pepper to taste

1. Put the onion and greens in a covered saucepan together with the water and put the lid on.

2. Steam or sauté the greens just until they're wilted. Every green is a little different, but this is about 5-7 minutes.

3. Take the greens out of the pot, put them on a plate, add some nice extra virgin olive oil and a little sea salt and pepper. Wow. Give it a try. Experiment with whatever your local market has available, and try different sea salts and oils. I like EVOO, but I also like sesame oil sometimes, especially when I serve this as a side with an Asian oriented dish such as the Orange Beef in this cookbook.

Hasselback Potato

In all fairness to my former spouse, he made a great Hasselback Potato. It has inspired this recipe. My digestive system doesn't handle cheese very well anymore (hmm....'wonder which came first, the spouse or the digestive problem....) but I seem to be okay with aged cheeses. I think the original recipe was made with Jarlsberg Swiss. I make mine with pecorino Romano because I like the taste, and also because since it's such a concentrated flavor, you use less of it. I think the recipe actually gets its name from the hotel, the Hasselbacken Hotel, in Stockholm, that started this idea originally.

1 medium sized raw long baking potato, peeled
1/8 cup freshly grated parmesan cheese
1/4 cup fine bread crumbs
1 Tbs. butter, melted
1/4 tsp. paprika
Sea salt to taste (I like the Yakima Applewood Smoked Sea salt from SaltWorks with this one)

1. Preheat oven to 450°.

2. Place the potato on a cutting board and cut a very thin slice from the bottom of the potato so that it is able to lie flat on your work surface. Place a wooden chopstick on each side of the potato, lengthwise. This is going to act as a brace so your knife doesn't go all the way through the potato, but starts the beginning of your "fan".

3. Using a sharp knife, make several slices across the potato about 1/4-inch apart, cutting straight down. The chopsticks will prevent the knife from cutting completely through the potato. Hold under cold, running water, while you gently fan the potato out and then allow the potato to dry for a few minutes before baking. If you like, you can prepare the potato in advance and leave it in a bowl of cold water until you're just about ready to bake it. The cold water will release some of the starch.

3. Brush the potato with the melted butter and wrap in foil. Bake for 15 minutes at 450°. Remove from the oven. Add the cheese and breadcrumbs and kind of push them down into the slats. Toss on some sea salt, re-wrap in the foil and return to the oven for another 15 minutes. Remove the potato, and remove the foil, and bake, uncovered, for the final 15 minutes. You may want to add another tablespoon of melted butter to the top before you serve it. It's up to you.

Mélange of Root Vegetables with Fennel

Use a Dutch oven for this one. You're going to do a little trick with the shallot and some sugar, and then add the vegetables and bake. Then, you'll toss everything with EVOO, essential oil, sea salt, and pepper.

1 shallot, chopped
1 Tbs. butter
1/4 tsp. sugar
1small turnip (purple preferred), scrubbed and cut into 1-inch pieces
1 small parsnip
1 small-med. sized carrot
1/2 – 1 bulb fennel, if desired
Sea salt and pepper to taste
1 Tbs. extra virgin olive oil
1 drop Young Living Essential Oils Fennel Oil

1. Oven at 375°

2. Over medium high heat, heat a Dutch oven or other skillet or something where you have a lid and you can cover and put it into the oven.

3. Add the butter and the sugar and cook to let the sugar caramelize just a tiny bit. Add the shallot and stir. Let the shallot work with the caramelizing sugar about 30 seconds or a minute while stirring. Do not leave the pan alone.

4. Now, add the other vegetables, clamp on the lid and put it in the oven. Do not touch it for 20 minutes.

5. Open the lid and check for doneness. Add another 10 minutes in the oven if necessary.

6. Remove from the oven to a large bowl once the vegetables are done. Add the EVOO, the one drop of fennel oil, sea salt and pepper to taste.

You can serve it like it is, or you can smash it on your plate, or you can dirty your food processor by pureeing it--your call. Enjoy.

Mélange of Zucchini, Carrot, Beet and Onion

This is a great accompaniment to any dish, or a nice dish served alone, or with rice or pasta, or alongside fried chicken or fish. One of the smoky sea sea salts available from SaltWorks, like Salish Alderwood smoked sea sea salt, can add just that little touch of difference.

1 Tbs. grape seed oil
1 small zucchini
1 carrot, boiled until just tender
1/2 - 1 beet, cooked and peeled
1/2 medium onion
1 Tbs. olive oil
Sea salt and pepper to taste

1. Dice the zucchini, carrot, beet and onion.

2. Heat grape seed oil over medium heat. Add the vegetables. Keeping them moving, cook until the zucchini is done.

3. Move the vegetables to a large bowl and toss until all the vegetables are lightly coated with the olive oil. Add sea salt and pepper to taste. Serve.

Oil Me Rosemary Sliced Delicata Squash

This recipe is really cool because, since you're not cooking this oil at all, you're getting the full health benefit of the rosemary, which is to improve mental clarity and concentration.

1 medium delicata squash
1 Tbs. grape seed oil
1 tsp. extra virgin olive oil
1 toothpick Young Living Essential Rosemary Oil *Sea salt and pepper to taste (I prefer the Murray River flake sea salt from SaltWorks)

*Remove the stopper a bottle of Rosemary Essential oil, insert a toothpick, remove it and swirl the toothpick around in the olive oil. This should give you a drop's worth without the chance of going overboard with it.

1. Preheat oven to 425°.

2. Slice the squash lengthwise and remove the seeds. If desired, rinse the seeds and bake alongside the squash. Now, cut the squash again, but this time in slices widthwise, about 1/2 inch widths.

3. Drop the rosemary oil onto a cookie sheet, and then the grape seed oil. Mix them together with your fingers, coating the cookie sheet.

4. Place the squash slices on the cookie sheet and bake for 10 minutes. The slices touching the pan will brown nicely.

5. Remove from the oven. Turn the slices over and return to oven to brown for another 10 minutes. By now, the squash should be tender and browned on both sides. If you think it needs more time, return to the oven for another 5 minutes, or for 5 minutes at a time until it's done. It's usually done by 20 minutes total, but every stove is just a little different.

6. Remove squash from the oven and brush on theEVOO, and sea salt and pepper to taste. Serve.

Roasted Root Vegetable with Balsamic Reduction

I like to make this one on the weekends, actually. I like to come straight home from Zestful Gardens, the organic garden I trade with on Saturdays vis-à-vis the Proctor Farmers Market, and make this. Sometimes I'll make 2 or 3 times this and then have it in a variety of incarnations throughout the week. But, as promised, I'm trying to keep every recipe down to a one-off, something you can whip up as a meal for one. Expand as your heart desires.

1 turnip, scrubbed and halved
2 carrots, scrubbed and halved
1 potato, scrubbed and quartered
1 small onion, maybe a Cipollini or two
Balsamic Reduction to taste (start with 1 tsp.)

1. Preheat oven to 450°.

2. Combine vegetables in an oven-safe dish and bake 20-40 minutes, until they're done. Drizzle with Balsamic Reduction and serve.

Another idea is to omit the potato, double the other ingredients, bake, slice thinly, add a standard cream sauce or roux of milk or milk substitute and flour or cornstarch, and layer between a couple of layers of those ready to use lasagna noodles. Add a couple dashes of nutmeg to the cream sauce, and you're all set.

This recipe is an excellent accompaniment to chicken, beef, or pork, or it stands alone well.

Rosemary Potatoes

This is a great way to use leftover potatoes. When you bake a potato, bake two instead and just cut to the chase on this one without need to go through the boiling. But, if you boil a potato, do so for about 10 minutes until it's just done, and not overdone. Let it cool. When I think about this at the last minute, I add ice cubes. I usually plan this ahead of time—but, not always.

1 cooked, cold potato (organic red potatoes are my favorites)
2 Tbs. grape seed oil
2 sprigs fresh rosemary
Sea salt and pepper to taste

1. Heat a large skillet over medium high heat. Add the grape seed oil, then the fresh rosemary. The rosemary kind of infuses the dish, and melts. You can take out the stem at the end.

2. Cut the potato into wedges. The number of wedges will of course depend on the size of the potato.

3. Add the potato wedges to the oil and cook on medium high heat until at least two of the three sides are brown. That's it! Add sea salt and pepper to taste and you're ready to plate it!

Twice-Baked Potato

1 baking potato, scrubbed and halved
1 Tbs. grape seed oil to coat the potato
Sea salt to taste (suggested: Yakima Applewood Smoked Sea Sea salt by SaltWorks)
1 Tbs. butter
1 drop Fennel Young Living Essential Oil
1/4 medium onion, finely diced
1 Tbs. extra virgin olive oil to mash inside the potato

1. Preheat oven to 450°F.

2. Scrub the potato, cut it in half, pour the grape seed oil into your hand and massage the potato with it.

3. Put the potato in a baking dish and dust with sea salt to suit your taste. I like to use Yakima Applewood Smoked Sea Sea salt by SaltWorks because that's the sea salt that has me fascinated now, but you can use any sea salt you like. Bake at 450° for 30-40 minutes until done, when you can stick a toothpick in it easily.

4. Remove the potato from the oven. Let it cool while you fix the filling.

5. Sautee the onion in the butter. Or, you can use water if you prefer to keep the oil content down. Over medium heat, just add the onion to the skillet, get the skillet warm, and add 2 Tbs. or so of water. Steam the onions until they're translucent. You can also add 1 tsp. of sugar--turbinado or brown--if you like, while they're steaming.

6. Scoop out the insides of the potato with a spoon and put them in a mixing bowl. Add the fennel oil, the onion, and the EVOO. Return the mixture to the potato jacket. Put the potatoes back in the oven and cook for another 10 minutes. Serve.

You may want to add 1/4 cup of parmesan or Romano cheese as well, or sprinkle a little over your potato at the end before serving.

Zesty Cauliflower

1 cup cauliflower florets
Zest and juice of 1/2 lemon per cup of cauliflower or use 1 drop of Young Living Essential Lemon Oil
1 cup vegetable or chicken broth
Sea salt and pepper to taste (Fleur de Sel works well in this recipe)
Drizzle of extra virgin olive oil if desired

1. Place florets in a covered saucepan with the vegetable broth, lemon and lemon juice.

2. Cover and steam until florets are done to your liking, about 5 - 10 minutes.

3. Drizzle with a little EVOO if desired, and add sea salt and pepper to taste.

Zucchini Chips

1 zucchini, sliced
1 egg plus 1 Tbs. water
Brown rice flour
3 Tbs. grape seed oil

1. Heat oil in cast iron pan.

2. Dredge zucchini in flour, then egg mixture, and then flour again. Return to pan.

3. Brown zucchini on both sides. Drain on paper towel and serve.

Soups

Easy Vegetable Soup
Radish Top Soup
Swedish Pasture Soup
White Bean and Kale Soup
White Bean and Pasta Soup

Easy Vegetable Soup

1 large carrot, finely chopped
About 3 tablespoons finely chopped onion
1 celery stalk, finely chopped
1 potato, finely chopped
1-32 ounce container vegetable or chicken stock
2 Tbs. grape seed oil
Pinch red pepper flakes

1. Heat the grape seed oil over medium heat, gently, just until the pan is warm, but not hot. Add the red pepper flakes and the vegetables. Let the vegetables sweat.

2. Add your stock to deglaze our pan, or you can use sweet or dry vermouth too, and then add the stock. Cover the pan and cook on medium heat for 10 minutes.

3. Remove cover and cook another twenty minutes, still on medium heat. Now you're done. You can add other vegetables if you want. You can add some fresh chicken or turkey breast, or leftover steak or roast. This is luscious. And, it freezes well.

Radish Top Soup

Are you still throwing away your radish tops? I did for years, actually--probably until I turned 52. Then, I met Valerie. Valerie and her daughter Holly own Zestful Gardens Organic Gardens and I've been buying my produce from them since I moved to Tacoma. Valerie told me about radish top soup.

1 bunch radish tops, rinsed and drained
1/2 medium onion, diced
1 cup chicken broth (I make mine from 1 tsp. Better than Bullion dissolved in a cup of boiling water)
1 Tbs. butter
Splash of lemon
Grated parmesan cheese
Sea salt and pepper to taste

1. Melt the butter in a small saucepan and add the onion.

2. Cook the onion until it's translucent and then add the chicken stock and the radish tops. Heat through and serve. Add a splash of lemon, a dusting of grated parmesan, and some sea salt and pepper before serving.

Swedish Pasture Soup / Ängemat

Traditionally, this soup was served in my mother-in-law's home accompanied by Swedish Hard Tack and cheese. Waffles or Swedish pancakes, or sometimes a Holland Baby (the baked version of a Swedish pancake where the batter is just put into a baking dish and baked off), was served afterwards, often accompanied as well by Swedish punch.

2 Tbs. butter
1/2 cup cauliflower
1 carrot, washed/scraped, and diced
1 stalk celery, thinly sliced
1/4 medium onion, diced
1-1/2 cups whole milk
1 egg, beaten with a fork

1. Melt 2 Tbs. butter in a 3-1/2 quarter saucepan. Add cauliflower, carrot, celery and onion and cook, stirring, over medium heat, until the vegetables are cooked through.

2. Add the milk. Scald--that's when you cook it until a skin forms and you remove the skin.

3. Remove from the heat. Add the beaten egg, stirring constantly. The egg will act as a thickener. Serve.

White Bean and Kale Soup

This particular soup seems to go over a little better when it's blended, topped with just a few drops of olive oil, some freshly grated Romano cheese and/or savory biscottis. You can make everything ahead of time, say, over the weekend when you have the time, and then just heat it up as needed. It freezes well too.

1-15 ounce can navy beans, great northern or cannellini beans, drained and rinse
2 Tbs. grape seed oil
Pinch cayenne pepper
2 stalks celery, coarsely chopped
½ onion, coarsely chopped
1 bunch kale, rinsed and drained
1-32 ounce container chicken or vegetable stock
Pecorino-Romano cheese, freshly grated, to taste

1. Heat the oil over medium high heat and add cayenne.

2. Add the onion and celery and allow them to sweat.

3. Add the beans, kale and chicken stock. Cover and cook over medium heat for twenty minutes. Remove from heat.

4. Blend in very small amounts, then return to pan to reheat the amount you want to use right away.

You can refrigerate the rest for three or four days, or freeze. I've kept mine in the frig for a week and it's been wonderful heated up, but it does have chicken stock so use your own judgment about your personal comfort level here.

I serve mine in a low bowl by adding a touch of extra virgin olive oil, a coating of freshly grated Pecorino-Romano cheese, and savory pepper biscotti (page 25) that I break up in the soup. It's a feast!

White Bean and Pasta Soup

When I was living in New York, before I became pregnant with my son, I stayed with my son's beautiful and caring extended Italian family. In those few delicious years between 18 and 22, when the world is your oyster, when you're just starting to explore the freedom of adulthood, that's when I was exposed to Pasta and Bean Soup and Pepper Biscotti for the first time. The soup was served piping hot and we broke up the Biscotti in the soup. The biscotti themselves were quite peppery and they added a real zing.

1-16 ounce can navy or other white beans, rinsed and drained
2 Tbs. extra virgin olive oil
Pinch red pepper flakes
½ cup onion, coarsely chopped
2 stalks celery, finely chopped
1-32 ounce container vegetable or chicken broth
½ cup ditalini pasta or other small pasta, cooked al dente
Fresh basil, thinly sliced
Freshly grated parmesan or Romano cheese, for garnish
Sea salt and pepper to taste

1. Heat olive oil over medium heat. Add red pepper flakes, onion and celery. Allow vegetables to sweat.

2. Once the vegetables are pretty much translucent, add the beans and chicken broth. Cook uncovered about twenty minutes.

To serve:

Place a little fresh basil in a soup bowl, and then add a couple of tablespoons of the cooked pasta, then add the soup to the bowl. Add some grated cheese and crumble pepper biscotti into the soup. Manga gysta Kai! (Eat with good appetite)

101 Dinner Ideas for One

Here are some meal ideas from me to you. A lot of the recipes, as you can see, are one-dish meals. If you're a person who likes her/his starch, then you may want to add some kind of rice or potato. Or, you may want to round out a meal with a green salad, or one of the salads in the book.

1. Carrot Pancakes served with Balsamic Reduction Whipped Cream and a side of crispy cooked bacon
2. Carrot, Pineapple, and Toasted Pecan Pancakes served with pork chop
3. Easy Vegetable Soup, followed by Greens Pancakes
4. Beef Stew for One and a small side salad
5. Cuban Fried Steak, Steamed Rice, Black Beans and Plantains
6. Easy Pot Roast served with a side of sliced tomatoes and cucumbers
7. Orange Beef served with brown jasmine rice and/or a side of cooked greens
8. Skewered Beef
9. Spicy Beef Curry served with Major Grey's Chutney and white or brown basmati rice
10. Zucchini Fritters with roasted beet and feta salad
11. Greens pancakes and a hamburger patty or burger equivalent like boca or black bean burger
12. Barbecued Chicken Pizza served with a side salad
13. Chicken a l'orange served with brown jasmine or wild rice
14. Chicken Chop Suey served with rice
15. Chinese Style Chicken Chow Mein served with brown or purple rice
16. Chicken Curry served with rice and a small side salad with champagne vinaigrette
17. Chicken Pot Pie
18. Chicken Roll-up with Prosciutto served with a small salad, or 2 cups of steamed chard
19. Chicken Stew with a Dumpling or Two
20. Green Beans with Chicken served with small boiled potato,

and/or a small salad

21. Is this Beef? Chicken, with a cup of leftover soup beforehand

22. Lemon Chicken served with a side of linguine

23. Maifun Chicken Salad for One served with a side of butternut squash

24. Mediterranean Chicken served with Rosemary Potatoes

25. Murray River Curry served with basmati rice and mango chutney

26. Murray River Mediterranean Chicken served with white jasmine rice

27. Quick and Easy Barbecued Chicken served with barbecued beans and cornbread

28. Poached Salmon with Lemon and Capers served with steamed broccoli

29. Chinese Style Tuna Casserole for One served with a small side salad and sesame vinaigrette

30. Fried Oysters with Ground Millet Coating, served with a side salad

31. Linguine with Clams served with lettuce and cucumber topped with lemon and olive oil

32. Mussels and Chips served with cucumber and carrot spears

33. Poached Salmon with Lemon served with a side of steamed kale with a touch of olive oil and a squirt of lemon

34. Steamed Clams with French bread served with a nice green salad

35. Swordfish and Mango Salsa served with a side of fresh steamed green beans

36. Tilapia with Panko Crust served with Green Beans with balsamic finish and a tomato slice

37. Artichoke Hearts, Sun-Dried Tomatoes and Penne Pasta served with a tossed green salad

38. Baked Penne with Kale served with tossed green salad or a slice of baked squash

39. Josie Pennello's Unforgettable Spaghetti Sauce served with a tossed salad and French bread

40. Mac and Cheese for One served with stewed tomatoes or

cooked beets (warm or cold, with a drizzle of balsamic)
41. Pasta Putanesca served with linguine and a side or romaine with balsamic vinaigrette
42. Pasta with Red Pepper and Peas served with a side of Delicata squash
43. Pasta with Prosciutto and Peppers served with a small salad of sliced kalamata olives, red onion and romaine lettuce topped with balsamic vinaigrette
44. Spaghetti Frittata served with a wilted chard salad
45. Larsson Hash served with homemade pickled beets and/or cooked green beans
46. Pork Chop with Cranberry Raisin Chutney served with a side of cooked beet greens or cooked kale topped with a little olive oil, balsamic vinegar, sea salt and pepper
47. Pork Chow Mein served with a side of miso soup (1 Tbs. Miso mixed with 1 cup water, cooked with 1/2 sliced green onion, but not boiled)
48. Pork Lo Mein served with the soba noodles
49. Pork Roast with Mint Rub served with Hasselback Potato and some steamed carrots
50. Pork Wrap with a cup of chicken broth to start
51. Simple Pork Ribs served with creamy polenta (1/3 cup cornmeal, 1 cup water, 1/4 tsp. sea salt, boiled until it's creamy--be careful of splattering toward the last, turn your heat down)
52. Baked Fennel served with a steak and maybe some spaghetti squash
53. Butternut Squash Soufflé for One served with sliced cold pork and a cooked beet
54. Fennel Flavored Risotto for 100 served with a small chef's salad of lettuces, meats and cheeses you have on hand
55. Fennel Flavored Risotto for 100 served with Lemon Chicken
56. Fried Rice served with Chinese Style Chicken Chow Mein |
57. Green Beans with balsamic finish served with a one or two egg omelet
58. Hasselback Potato served with a nice little New York steak topped with sautéed mushrooms, and aside salad
59. Hasselback Potato served with sautéed greens with onions

and some kind of dinner sausage

60. Mélange of Root Vegetables with balsamic reduction served with roast beef

61. Mélange of Zucchini, Carrot, Beet and Onion served with sautéed tilapia cooked in coconut oil and topped off with a splash of lime

62. Oil Me Rosemary Sliced Delicata Squash served with a salmon filet and some fresh green beans

63. Roasted Root Vegetables with Balsamic Reduction served with brown rice

64. Rosemary Potato served with Chicken Roll-up with Prosciutto and a small green salad

65. Twice Baked Potato served with a salmon filet and a cup of cooked greens

66. Zesty Cauliflower served with a salmon filet and a cup of cooked greens

67. Zesty Cauliflower served with a tilapia filet and a tossed green salad

68. Zucchini Chips served with a hamburger, boca or black bean burger

69. Zucchini Chips served with penne pasta topped with extra virgin olive oil, parmesan cheese, sea salt and pepper

70. Easy Vegetable Soup served with crackers and cheese or a tossed green salad

71. Easy Vegetable Soup served with pepper biscotti and a cucumber salad (sliced cucumber and onion in a champagne vinaigrette)

72. Radish Top Soup served with a grilled cheese sandwich

73. Swedish Pasture Soup served with hard tack and cheese

74. Swedish Pasture Soup followed by a waffle or pancake

75. White Bean and Kale Soup served with Peppery Biscotti and a side salad of sliced kalamata olives, romaine and red onion topped with balsamic vinegar

76. White bean and Pasta Soup served with rustic Italian bread and celery stuffed with cream cheese

77. Beet Green Frittata served with a Massaged Kale Salad

78. Beet Pancakes with Coconut sour cream and Chives served

with Radish Top Soup as a starter

79. Egg Foo Young for One served with Pork Lo Mein (you can leave out the pork)

80. I Have Too Many Greens This Week Pie served with a small green salad

81. Metropolitan Pizza served with cucumber spears

82. Tofu Omelet served with fried diced potatoes

83. Vege Sushi Roll served with miso soup

84. Vegetable Coconut Curry with Egg served with Fried Banana and basmati rice

85. Zucchini Parmesan with Tomato Sauce served with spaghetti topped with a little extra virgin olive oil, sea salt and pepper to taste, and some fresh basil

86. Roasted Beet and Feta Salad served with baked salmon filet (15-20 minutes in a 350° oven)

87. Raw Beet and Apple Salad with Pine Nuts and Arugula served with a juice New York steak

88. Raw Beet and Apple Salad with Pine Nuts and Arugula served with Butternut Squash Soufflé for One

89. Apple and Carrot Salad with Toasted Pecans served with a bison burger

90. Apple and Carrot Salad with Toasted Pecans served with bacon and scrambled eggs

91. Apple and Carrot Salad with Toasted Pecans served with baked acorn squash

92. Wilted Chard Salad served with a pork chop

93. Wilted Chard Salad served with a dish of penne pasta cooked with 1/2 a tomato

94. Massaged Kale Salad served with a grilled cheese sandwich

95. Tossed Fall Vegetable Salad served with a tuna sandwich

96. Tossed Fall Vegetable Salad served with a juicy steak

97. Tossed Fall Vegetable Salad served with Baked Penne with Kale

98. Tofu Omelet served with a tossed green salad

99. Zucchini Parmesan with Tomato Sauce served with a salad of romaine, sliced kalamata olives and red onion, in a balsamic vinaigrette

100. Greens Pancakes served with crispy bacon
101. Greens Pancakes served with a mixed greens salad with tomato, cucumber, red onion if desired, and toasted pine nuts

Referenced in this Volume

Eat Right for Your Blood Type
by Dr. Peter J. D'Adamo with Catherine Whitney

The Bonus Years Diet"
Dr. Ralph Felder, MD, PhD.

The Amazing Liver & Gallbladder Flush
By Andreas Moritz

Gluten-Free Baking for Dummies®
By Jean M. Layton and Linda Larsen

www.Gluten-FreeGirlandtheChef.com

www.Young Living.com
My member number: 1019821

Index

101 Meals for One, 170
Apple and Carrot Salad with Toasted Pecans, 30
Artichoke Hearts, Sun-Dried Tomatoes and Penne Pasta, 112
Baked Fennel, 140
Baked Penne with Kale, 113
Baked Salmon with Lemon and Capers, 86
Balsamic Reduction Whipped Coconut Cream, 41
Balsamic Vinaigrette, 42
Balsamic Vinegar Reduction, 40
Barbecued Chicken Pizza, 60
Beef Stew for One, 50
Beet Green Frittata, 124
Beet Pancakes with Coconut Sour Cream and Chives, 16
Broccoli Bake, 141
Butternut Squash Soufflé for One, 142
Carrot, Pineapple and Toasted Walnut Pancakes with Balsamic Vinegar Reduction, 18
Cauliflower Steaks, 143
Champagne Vinaigrette salad dressing, 43
Chicken a l'orange, 61
Chicken Chop Suey, 63

Chicken Curry, 62
Chicken Pot Pie, 68
Chicken Roll-up with Prosciutto, 70
Chicken Stew with a Dumpling or Two, 65
Chinese Style Chicken Chow Mein, 67
Chinese Style Tuna Casserole for One, 87
Coconut sour cream, 44
Cranberry Apple Chutney, 45
Cuban Fried Steak (Bistec de Palomilla), 52
Easy Pot Roast for One, 54
Easy Vegetable Soup, 164
Egg Foo Young for One, 125
Fennel flavored risotto for 100, 144
Fried Oysters with Ground Millet Coating, 88
Fried rice, 146
Gluten-Free Pizza Dough, 127
Green Beans with Balsamic Finish, 147
Green Beans with Chicken, 71
Greens Pancakes, 22
Greens Sautéed or Steamed with Onion, 148
Hasselback Potato, 149
I Have Too Many Greens This Week Pie, 128

Is this Beef? Chicken, 72
Josie Pennello's
    Unforgettable Spaghetti
    Sauce, 114
Larsson Hash, 100
Lemon Chicken, 73
Lemony Pancakes with
    Grilled Shrimp, 89
Linguine with Clams, 91
Mac and Cheese for One, 116
Maifun Chicken Salad for
    One, 75
Massaged Kale Salad with
    Creamy Tahini Miso
    Dressing, 31
Massaged Kale Salad with
    Tahini and Lemon
    Dressing, 32
Mediterranean Chicken, 76
Mélange of Root
    Vegetables, 151
Mélange of Zucchini,
    Carrot, Beet and Onion, 153
Metropolitan Pizza, 130
Murray River Curry, 77
Murray River
    Mediterranean Chicken, 79
Mussels and Chips, 92
Oil Me Rosemary Sliced
    Delicata Squash, 154
Orange and Cardamom
    Biscotti, 23
Orange Beef, 55

Orange Carrot Pancakes
    with Balsamic Reduction
    Whipped Coconut
    Cream, 18
Pasta Putanesca, 117
Pasta with Prosciutto and
    Peppers, 119
Pasta with Red Pepper and
    Peas, 118
Peanut sauce, 46
Peppery Biscotti, 25
Poached salmon with
    Lemon and Capers, 93
Pork Chop with Cranberry
    Apple Chutney, 101
Pork Chow Mein, 103
Pork Lo Mein, 105
Pork Roast with Mint Rub, 106
Pork wrap, 107
Quick and Easy Barbecued
    Chicken, 81
Radish Top Soup, 165
Raw Beet and Apple Salad
    with Pine nuts and
    Arugula, 33
Raw Beet Pancakes with
    Oregano and Balsamic
    Reduction, 26
Roasted Beet and Feta
    Salad, 34
Roasted Root Vegetable
    with Balsamic Reduction, 155
Rosemary Potatoes, 156
Sesame Rice Vinaigrette
    salad dressing, 47

Simple Pork Ribs, 109
Skewered Beef, 56
Spaghetti Frittata, 120
Spicy Beef Curry, 57
Steamed Clams with French bread, 94
Swedish Pasture Soup / Ängemat, 166
Swordfish with Mango Salsa, 95
Tilapia in Panko Crust, 96
Tofu Omelet, 131
Tossed Fall Vegetable Salad, 35
Twice-Baked Potato, 157
Vege Sushi Rolls, 132
Vegetable Coconut Curry with Egg, 134
White Bean and Kale Soup, 167
White Bean and Pasta Soup, 168
Wilted Chard Salad, 36
Zesty Cauliflower, 159
Zucchini Chips, 160
Zucchini Fritter, 27
Zucchini Parmesan, 136

Made in the USA
San Bernardino, CA
04 October 2014